Published by Lulu
www.lulu.com
First Edition
ISBN: 979-8-234-05296-4

SHIELDING INTELLIGENCE

A DEEP DIVE INTO SECURING AI SYSTEMS

Preface

Artificial intelligence is no longer something on the horizon. It is already embedded in the systems that make decisions about money, health, risk, and access. As its presence grows, so does the impact of the choices behind it. Those choices are not abstract. They are made by people.

This book exists because there is a gap between how quickly AI is advancing and how thoughtfully it is being secured.

Most conversations about AI focus on capability. What it can do. How fast it can scale. How much it can replace or optimize. Far fewer conversations deal with the reality that these systems are often fragile in ways that are not obvious. They learn from data that can be manipulated. They make decisions that are difficult to explain. They operate inside organizations that are not always designed to manage that level of complexity.

Security in this context cannot be treated as a layer added at the end. It has to be understood as part of the system itself. Technical design, organizational structure, and human behavior all interact in ways that create both strength and vulnerability. You cannot address one without considering the others.

What becomes clear is that AI security is not owned by one team or one function. It is carried across roles. Engineers, product leaders, risk partners, executives, and practitioners all influence outcomes, whether they realize it or not. The systems reflect the decisions that were made along the way.

This book is meant to give you a way to think about that responsibility.

It walks through how AI systems are built, where they are most vulnerable, and why traditional approaches to security fall short. It also looks beyond the technical layer into how organizations operate, how decisions get made, and how culture shapes what is prioritized and what is ignored.

You will not find a promise of perfect security here because it simply does not exist. What does exist is the ability to make systems better, incrementally and consistently. Small decisions add up. Over time, they shape whether systems can be trusted.

The future of AI will not be determined by the technology alone. It will be shaped by the people building it, questioning it, and deciding how it is used. That is the thread running through every chapter.

If you are working in or around AI, this applies to you.

The responsibility is shared. The work is ongoing. What you choose to do with it matters.

Introduction

Artificial intelligence has moved beyond the realm of emerging technology to become foundational infrastructure for modern society. AI systems now drive decisions in healthcare diagnostics, financial transactions, autonomous vehicle navigation, criminal justice sentencing, and countless other domains that directly impact human lives. This ubiquity poses unprecedented security challenges, requiring entirely new defensive strategies and governance frameworks.

This book provides a comprehensive exploration of AI security, from the technical foundations of how AI systems work and why they are vulnerable, through the adversarial threat landscape, secure development practices, ethical and regulatory considerations, robust defensive techniques, industry-specific implementations, advanced emerging technologies, organizational maturity, governance frameworks, and the path forward for practitioners and organizations alike.

Organized across ten chapters, the text progresses from foundational concepts to advanced strategies. Chapters One through Three establish the technical groundwork: core AI architectures and their inherent vulnerabilities, the adversarial threat landscape encompassing adversarial examples, data poisoning, model extraction, and privacy attacks, and a complete framework for developing secure AI systems from inception. Chapter Four broadens the lens to address ethics, fairness, and the rapidly evolving regulatory landscape. Chapter Five delivers practical defensive techniques—adversarial training, input validation, model hardening, ensemble methods, certified defenses, and incident response. Chapter

Six translates these principles into industry-specific implementations across healthcare, finance, manufacturing, retail, and transportation.

The final four chapters look ahead. Chapter Seven examines advanced technologies including quantum computing, privacy-preserving machine learning, and AI-driven cybersecurity. Chapter Eight addresses organizational maturity, evolving standards, and building effective security programs. Chapter Nine synthesizes the key insights across all chapters and charts a clear path forward for individuals and organizations. Chapter Ten introduces a governance framework that moves beyond traditional perimeter security to address the deeper challenge of controlling what AI systems do when functioning exactly as designed.

Each chapter includes learning objectives, real-world case studies, key takeaways, and reflection questions designed to bridge understanding and action. Whether you are a security professional, AI practitioner, organizational leader, policymaker, or researcher, this book equips you with the knowledge and frameworks necessary to navigate the complex and evolving landscape of AI security.

Table of Contents

Introduction .... **vii**

Chapter One: The Foundation of AI Security **1**

1.1 Decoding AI Architecture 2
1.2 The Evolution of AI and Emerging Security Paradigms 6
1.3 The AI Development Lifecycle and Attack Surfaces 8
1.4 Fundamental Vulnerabilities in AI Systems 12
1.5 Toward Secure AI Systems 16

Chapter Two: The Adversarial Threat Landscape **23**

2.1 Adversarial Examples: Exploiting Decision Boundaries 24
2.2 Data Poisoning: Corrupting the Learning Process 28
2.3 Model Extraction: Intellectual Property Theft 32
2.4 Privacy Attacks: Extracting Sensitive Information 34
2.5 Integrity and Availability Attacks 37
2.6 Emerging Threats 39
2.7 Real-World Attack Case Studies 41

Chapter Three: Developing Secure AI Systems **47**

3.1 Security-by-Design Principles 48
3.2 Secure Data Management 54
3.3 Secure Model Development 58
3.4 Security Testing and Validation 61
3.5 Secure Deployment 63
3.6 Continuous Security Improvement 66

Chapter Four: Ethics, Fairness, and Regulatory Compliance .. **75**

4.1 Ethical Foundations of AI Security 76
4.2 Fairness in AI Systems 79
4.3 The Regulatory Landscape 82
4.4 Building Accountable AI Systems 85
4.5 Privacy Regulation and AI 87

4.6 Case Studies in Ethics and Compliance........ 89
4.7 Compliance Implementation Strategies........ 92

Chapter Five: Building Robust Defenses for AI Systems......... 99

5.1 Adversarial Training........ 100
5.2 Input Validation and Sanitization........ 104
5.3 Model Hardening Techniques........ 107
5.4 Ensemble Methods........ 109
5.5 Certified Defenses........ 111
5.6 Runtime Monitoring and Detection........ 113
5.7 Defense Against Specific Attack Types........ 116
5.8 Defense Evaluation and Testing........ 118
5.9 Incident Response for AI Systems........ 120

Chapter Six: Industry-Specific AI Security Implementation . 127

6.1 Healthcare........ 128
6.2 Financial Services........ 134
6.3 Manufacturing and Industrial IoT........ 139
6.4 Retail and E-Commerce........ 144
6.5 Transportation and Autonomous Systems........ 148
6.6 Cross-Industry Considerations........ 153

Chapter Seven: Advanced Technologies and Future Directions..159

7.1 Quantum Computing and AI Security........ 160
7.2 Privacy-Preserving Machine Learning........ 164
7.3 Explainability for Security........ 170
7.4 AI-Driven Cybersecurity........ 173
7.5 Emerging Threats........ 177
7.6 Future-Proofing AI Security........ 181

Chapter Eight: The Future of AI Security........ 189

8.1 Organizational Maturity in AI Security........ 190
8.2 The Evolving Standards and Regulatory Ecosystem........ 196
8.3 Building Effective AI Security Programs........ 201
8.4 Cross-Functional Collaboration........ 208
8.5 Long-Term Trends Shaping AI Security........ 214
8.6 Preparing for the Future........ 219

Chapter Nine: The Path Forward 231

9.1 The Essential Synthesis 232
9.2 Critical Challenges Ahead 236
9.3 Reasons for Optimism 240
9.4 Your Role in the Future 242
9.5 A Vision for 2035 246
9.6 The Call to Action 249
9.7 The Final Word 251

Chapter Ten: AI Governance Beyond Perimeter Security.............

10.1 The Accountability Vacuum.. 263
10.2 Decision Sovereignty Mapping.. 265
10.3 From Transparency to Intelligibility... 268
10.4 Adversarial Thinking as Governance Discipline.......................... 271
10.5 Governance Architecture 274
10.6 Implementation Strategies 277
10.7 Case Studies in AI Governance 279

References 287

1

The Foundation of AI Security

Learning Objectives

By the end of this chapter, you will:

- Understand the core architectures that power modern artificial intelligence systems
- Recognize the fundamental security challenges inherent in AI design
- Identify critical vulnerability points across the AI development lifecycle
- Grasp how historical AI evolution shapes current security paradigms
- Appreciate why traditional security approaches fail against AI-specific threats

Introduction: The Security Imperative

Artificial intelligence has transcended its status as an emerging technology to become foundational infrastructure for modern society. AI systems now make decisions about healthcare diagnoses, financial transactions, autonomous vehicle navigation, and criminal justice sentencing. This ubiquity creates unprecedented security challenges that demand new defensive strategies.

Traditional cybersecurity focused on protecting static systems with defined boundaries. AI security requires a paradigm shift. We must protect systems that learn, adapt, and evolve. We must secure models whose decision boundaries shift with new data. We must defend against attacks that exploit the very learning mechanisms that make AI powerful.

This chapter establishes the conceptual foundation necessary for understanding AI security. We begin with the technical architectures that define modern AI, then examine the unique vulnerabilities these architectures introduce. Throughout, we maintain focus on practical security implications rather than theoretical abstractions.

1.1 Decoding AI Architecture

The Intelligence Spectrum

Artificial intelligence exists along a spectrum of capability. At one end, we find narrow AI systems designed for specific tasks. These systems excel within constrained domains but cannot generalize beyond their training objectives. At the spectrum's opposite end, we envision artificial general intelligence (AGI) that matches or exceeds human cognitive flexibility across all domains.

Current security challenges center on narrow AI. These systems dominate real-world deployments despite their limitations. A medical diagnosis AI cannot drive vehicles. A fraud detection system cannot translate languages. This specialization creates very focused attack surfaces that adversaries will study and exploit.

Narrow AI operates through pattern recognition rather than understanding. Consider an image classifier trained to identify cats. The system learns statistical correlations between pixel patterns and the "cat" label. It does not understand what makes an animal a cat. This gap between pattern matching and comprehension creates fundamental vulnerabilities we will explore throughout this book.

The Learning Paradigm Shift

Modern AI derives its power from machine learning rather than explicit programming. Traditional software follows deterministic rules written by programmers. Machine learning systems infer their own rules from data. This inversion of the programming paradigm introduces novel security challenges.

Three primary learning paradigms dominate current AI systems:

Supervised Learning trains models on labeled examples. The system learns to map inputs to outputs by studying examples with known correct answers. A spam filter learns from emails labeled as spam or legitimate. This approach dominates in applications where abundant labeled data is available. From a security perspective, supervised learning creates a dependency on the integrity of the training data. Adversaries who corrupt training labels can systematically compromise model behavior.

Unsupervised Learning discovers patterns in unlabeled data. These systems identify structure without explicit guidance about what to find. Clustering algorithms group similar data points. Anomaly detection systems identify unusual patterns that deviate from normal behavior. Security applications frequently employ unsupervised learning because attacks often appear as anomalies rather than known patterns. However, this same property makes unsupervised systems vulnerable to adversaries who gradually shift what appears "normal."

Reinforcement Learning trains agents through interaction with environments. The agent takes actions, receives rewards or penalties, and adjusts its strategy to maximize cumulative reward. This approach powers game-playing AI and autonomous systems. Reinforcement learning introduces unique security challenges because adversaries can manipulate the environment or reward signals to induce desired behaviors.

Each paradigm carries distinct vulnerability profiles. Understanding these differences enables targeted defensive strategies rather than generic security measures.

Neural Architecture Foundations

Neural networks provide the computational substrate for most modern AI systems. These architectures draw inspiration from biological neural systems but diverge significantly in implementation details. Understanding neural network fundamentals illuminates why certain attacks succeed and how defenses must adapt.

A neural network consists of interconnected computational units called neurons. These units transform input signals through nonlinear activation functions and pass results to subsequent layers. The network's behavior emerges from millions or billions of individual transformations coordinated through learned connection weights.

Feedforward Networks process information in a single direction, from input to output. These architectures excel at pattern recognition tasks where spatial or temporal relationships do not dominate. Security-critical applications include malware detection and spam filtering. Feedforward networks prove vulnerable to adversarial examples that exploit the geometric properties of high-dimensional decision boundaries.

Convolutional Neural Networks specialize in processing grid-structured data, such as images. Convolutional layers apply filters that detect local patterns regardless of position. This translation invariance makes CNNs powerful for computer vision tasks. Security applications include facial recognition and document analysis. CNNs introduce new attack surfaces, as adversaries can craft imperceptible perturbations that drastically alter network outputs.

Recurrent Neural Networks maintain an internal state that evolves as they process sequential inputs. This memory mechanism enables modeling temporal dependencies in data such as text or time series. Long Short-Term Memory (LSTM) and Gated Recurrent Unit (GRU) architectures address the vanishing gradient problem that plagued earlier recurrent designs. Security-critical applications include fraud detection and intrusion detection systems that analyze event sequences. RNNs face unique vulnerabilities from adversaries who inject carefully timed inputs that corrupt the internal state.

Transformer Architectures revolutionized natural language processing and are increasingly impacting other domains. Transformers process entire sequences simultaneously using attention mechanisms that weigh the importance of different input elements. Models like BERT and GPT demonstrate remarkable language-understanding capabilities. From a security perspective, transformers introduce massive parameter counts (billions of weights), creating extensive attack surfaces. Their attention mechanisms can be manipulated to ignore security-critical information or focus on adversarial distractors.

Graph Neural Networks extend deep learning to graph-structured data representing relationships between entities. These architectures prove valuable for analyzing social networks, molecular structures, and computer networks. Security applications include detecting coordinated disinformation campaigns and identifying malicious network activity patterns. GNNs are vulnerable to adversaries who strategically modify graph structure or node features to evade detection.

Each architecture makes different trade-offs between expressiveness, computational efficiency, and interpretability. These trade-offs directly impact security. More complex architectures often achieve better performance but become harder to analyze for vulnerabilities. Understanding architectural properties guides the selection of appropriate defensive strategies.

1.2 The Evolution of AI and Emerging Security Paradigms

Wave Theory of AI Development

AI development has progressed through distinct waves, each characterized by distinct capabilities and, consequently, different security challenges. Understanding this evolution clarifies why current defensive approaches emerged and where future vulnerabilities may appear.

The Symbolic Era (1950s-1980s) focused on explicit knowledge representation and logical reasoning. Expert systems encoded human knowledge as rules. These systems were transparent but brittle. Security challenges remained limited because capabilities were constrained. Adversaries could study rule bases but faced significant effort to craft inputs that exploited logical flaws.

The Statistical Era (1990s-2010s) embraced machine learning methods that learned patterns from data rather than encoding explicit rules. Support vector machines, random forests, and early neural networks demonstrated superior performance on practical tasks. This shift introduced new vulnerabilities. Models became black boxes whose decision logic resisted inspection. Training data poisoning emerged as attackers learned to corrupt learning processes.

The Deep Learning Era (2012-2020) leveraged neural networks with many layers processing hierarchical feature representations. Deep learning achieved breakthrough performance on perception tasks like image and speech recognition. Massive datasets and computational resources enabled training models with billions of parameters. This era brought AI security into sharp focus as systems deployed at scale proved vulnerable to adversarial attacks, data poisoning, and privacy violations.

The Foundation Model Era (2020-present) introduced models pre-trained on vast unlabeled datasets that can be adapted to many downstream tasks. Large language models, vision transformers, and multimodal systems demonstrate emergent capabilities not explicitly programmed. Security challenges multiply as these powerful models become widely accessible. Adversaries can fine-tune foundation models for malicious purposes. The models' vast knowledge bases introduce risks of memorizing and regurgitating sensitive training data.

Current Landscape Analysis

Today's AI security landscape reflects several converging trends:

Democratization of AI through open-source frameworks and pre-trained models lowers barriers to entry. Organizations without extensive AI expertise can deploy sophisticated systems. This accessibility accelerates innovation but also empowers adversaries. Attackers leverage the same tools and models to craft sophisticated attacks.

Edge Deployment moves AI inference from centralized clouds to distributed devices. This shift reduces latency and protects privacy but introduces new security challenges. Edge devices often lack robust security mechanisms. Physical access enables new attack vectors. Model extraction becomes easier when attackers control the execution environment.

Federated Learning enables training models across distributed data without centralizing information. Healthcare consortia and financial institutions adopt federated approaches to preserve privacy while benefiting from collaborative learning. Security challenges include Byzantine attacks, where malicious participants corrupt the global model, and privacy attacks that reconstruct training data from model updates.

AI-as-a-Service platforms expose model capabilities through APIs. Organizations train complex models and monetize them by selling prediction services. This model introduces intellectual property concerns. Adversaries can query models systematically to steal functionality or extract sensitive training information.

Autonomous Systems deploy AI in safety-critical applications with minimal human oversight. Self-driving vehicles, automated trading systems, and AI-powered medical devices make decisions affecting human lives and financial stability. Security failures in these contexts carry catastrophic consequences.

These trends shape the threat landscape. Defenses must address distributed deployments, service-oriented architectures, and safety-critical applications simultaneously.

1.3 The AI Development Lifecycle and Attack Surfaces

From Data to Deployment

AI systems progress through distinct development phases. Each phase introduces specific security considerations and potential vulnerabilities. Comprehensive defense requires securing the entire lifecycle rather than focusing solely on deployed models.

Data Collection begins the process. Training data may originate from sensors, user interactions, web scraping, or purchased datasets. Quality and representativeness determine model capabilities. From a security perspective, this phase proves highly vulnerable. Adversaries can introduce poisoned samples at the source. Supply chain attacks inject malicious data before organizations even acquire it. Once corrupted data enters the pipeline, detecting manipulation becomes exponentially harder.

Data Curation involves cleaning, labeling, and organizing collected data. Human annotators assign labels that guide supervised learning. Data augmentation techniques synthetically expand training sets. Security challenges include label-flipping attacks, in which annotators (malicious or deceived) assign incorrect labels. Augmentation can amplify poisoned samples throughout the dataset. Quality control mechanisms must balance efficiency and security, often resulting in trade-offs.

Feature Engineering transforms raw data into representations suitable for learning algorithms. Domain experts craft features that encode relevant information for the target task. This process introduces implicit assumptions about what matters. Adversaries who understand these assumptions can craft attacks that exploit feature blind spots. Automated feature learning through neural networks reduces but does not eliminate this vulnerability.

Model Training optimizes model parameters to minimize errors on training data. This computationally intensive phase may take days or weeks for large models. Security concerns include training-time backdoor attacks that embed hidden triggers. Resource exhaustion attacks target the training infrastructure. Side-channel attacks potentially extract information from training computations. Ensuring training integrity requires secure hardware, monitored environments, and robust validation.

Model Validation assesses the trained model's performance on held-out test data. Standard metrics like accuracy, precision, and recall quantify capabilities. However, traditional validation focuses on average-case performance. Security-aware validation must also assess worst-case behavior. Robustness testing evaluates performance under adversarial perturbations. Fairness audits assess bias in predictions across demographic groups. Privacy testing assesses resistance to membership inference attacks.

Model Deployment transitions validated models into production environments. This phase introduces new attack surfaces. Deployed models face direct adversary interaction. Serving infrastructure must handle potentially malicious queries. Model monitoring systems must detect anomalous behavior without creating excessive false alarms. Version control becomes critical as models update to maintain accuracy on shifting data distributions.

Model Monitoring continues after deployment. Production models face data drift as real-world distributions evolve. Concept drift occurs when the relationship between inputs and outputs changes. Adversarial drift happens when attackers systematically probe for weaknesses. Monitoring systems must distinguish benign distribution shifts from attacks while maintaining low false-positive rates to avoid alert fatigue.

Each phase presents opportunities for both defensive measures and adversarial exploitation. Effective security strategies address the full lifecycle rather than treating deployment as the sole security perimeter.

The Attack Surface Taxonomy

AI systems expose multiple attack surfaces that adversaries can target:

Data Pipeline Attacks target the information supply chain feeding AI systems. These attacks prove particularly insidious because they occur before model training begins. Poisoned data integrated into training sets creates persistent vulnerabilities that defenses struggle to detect. Supply chain attacks at data collection points can compromise entire model families trained on corrupted datasets.

Training Process Attacks manipulate the learning procedure itself. Backdoor attacks embed triggers that cause specific behaviors when activated. Hyperparameter manipulation corrupts model optimization. Byzantine attacks in distributed training inject malicious gradients. These attacks require less access than data pipeline attacks but still occur before deployment, making detection challenging.

Inference Attacks target deployed models through carefully crafted inputs. Adversarial examples add imperceptible perturbations that cause misclassification. Evasion attacks modify malicious content to bypass detection. Prompt injection attacks manipulate large language models to ignore safety constraints. These attacks occur in production, where defenses must operate in real time.

Model Extraction Attacks steal intellectual property by querying deployed models and training substitute models that replicate functionality. Query-based extraction systematically explores decision boundaries. Equation-solving attacks directly compute model parameters for simpler architectures. These attacks exploit the model-as-a-service paradigm that monetizes AI capabilities.

Privacy Attacks extract information about training data from model behavior. Membership inference determines whether specific examples appeared in training data. Attribute inference deduces sensitive properties of training examples. Model inversion reconstructs training data from model parameters. These attacks violate user privacy and potentially expose confidential information.

Availability Attacks deny service by overwhelming computational resources. Adversarial examples can trigger worst-case complexity for certain algorithms. Resource exhaustion attacks submit expensive queries that consume processing capacity. These attacks parallel traditional denial-of-service but exploit AI-specific computational patterns.

Understanding this taxonomy enables systematic threat modeling. Organizations can identify which attack surfaces their specific deployments expose and prioritize defenses accordingly.

1.4 Fundamental Vulnerabilities in AI Systems

The Brittleness Problem

Neural networks exhibit a fundamental brittleness that has no parallel in traditional software. Models that achieve superhuman performance on benchmark datasets can fail catastrophically when presented with inputs that differ slightly from the training distribution. This brittleness stems from the high-dimensional geometry of neural network decision boundaries.

Consider an image classifier that distinguishes between hundreds of object categories. The model learns to partition a high-dimensional space representing possible images. Decision boundaries separate regions assigned to different classes. In high-dimensional spaces, these boundaries lie extremely close to typical data points. Mathematically imperceptible perturbations can cross decision boundaries and trigger misclassification.

This geometric property enables adversarial examples. Attackers add carefully calculated noise to inputs that push them across decision boundaries. The perturbations remain imperceptible to humans but dramatically change model predictions. A stop sign with adversarial stickers might be classified as a speed limit sign by an autonomous vehicle's vision system.

The brittleness problem extends beyond adversarial examples. Models struggle with out-of-distribution inputs that differ from training data in ways humans consider minor. An image classifier trained on daytime photos may fail on nighttime images. A natural language system trained on formal writing may misinterpret casual speech. This lack of robustness creates security vulnerabilities that adversaries can exploit systematically.

The Opacity Challenge

Deep neural networks function as black boxes. Even experts struggle to explain why models make specific predictions. This opacity has several root causes:

Distributed Representations encode information across millions of parameters rather than in human-interpretable symbols. No single weight determines model behavior. Predictions emerge from complex interactions between many simple computations.

Nonlinear Transformations through multiple layers create highly complex functions that resist analysis. Small input changes can trigger cascading effects through the network architecture.

High Dimensionality prevents visualization and intuition. Humans cannot mentally picture spaces with thousands or even millions of dimensions in which neural computations occur.

This opacity creates security challenges:

Verification Becomes Impractical. Traditional software can be formally verified against specifications. Neural networks resist such analysis. We cannot prove that models will never produce specific incorrect outputs.

Debugging Requires Different Approaches. When neural networks fail, identifying root causes proves difficult. Traditional debugging examines code execution step by step. Neural network debugging must analyze distributed statistical patterns.

Auditing Demands New Tools. Regulatory compliance often requires demonstrating system properties like fairness or privacy preservation. Black box models make such demonstrations challenging without specialized explainability techniques.

Backdoors Hide Effectively. Attackers can embed malicious functionality in models without creating obvious artifacts. The distributed nature of neural representations allows backdoors to disperse across many parameters.

Addressing opacity requires developing interpretability techniques that expose model decision processes. However, interpretability often comes at the expense of performance. More interpretable models may prove less accurate or efficient.

The Data Dependency

AI systems' capabilities derive entirely from their training data. This fundamental dependency creates critical vulnerabilities:

Garbage In, Garbage Out amplified. Traditional software with bad inputs produces bad outputs, but the software itself remains correct. Machine learning with corrupted training data produces fundamentally flawed models. The corruption persists even with clean operational inputs.

Bias Inheritance means models absorb and amplify biases present in training data. Historical hiring data that reflects discrimination trains models that perpetuate it. Facial recognition systems trained on unrepresentative datasets perform worse on underrepresented groups.

Privacy Leakage occurs because models memorize aspects of training data. Careful querying can extract information about specific training examples. Large language models occasionally regurgitate verbatim text from training documents, potentially exposing sensitive information.

A Distribution Shift Vulnerability occurs when deployment data differs from training data. Models optimized for training distributions may behave unpredictably on shifted distributions. Adversaries who understand the properties of training data can craft attacks that exploit these differences.

Data dependency means that securing AI requires securing the entire data pipeline from collection through processing. Defense cannot focus solely on protecting deployed models.

The Arms Race Dynamic

AI security exhibits an asymmetric arms race between attackers and defenders. This dynamic arises from fundamental properties of machine learning:

Attack Efficiency: Adversaries need only find one successful attack vector. Defenders must protect against all possible attacks. This asymmetry favors attackers in resource-constrained environments.

Transferability: Attacks developed against one model often transfer to other models. Adversarial examples crafted for one image classifier frequently fool different classifiers. This property allows attackers to develop attacks offline against surrogate models before targeting production systems.

Adaptive Attacks: Defenders who publicize defensive mechanisms enable attackers to adapt. Published defense papers provide roadmaps for circumventing protections. This contrasts with traditional security, where Kerckhoffs's principle states that security should not depend on the secrecy of defensive mechanisms.

Evolutionary Pressure: Each defensive innovation spurs the development of more sophisticated attacks. Adversarial training produces models more robust to known attack patterns but potentially more vulnerable to novel attacks. This creates an endless cycle of measure and countermeasure.

Economic Incentives: The value of successfully attacking AI systems often exceeds the cost of defending against them. Financial fraud, intellectual property theft, and manipulation of decision-making systems provide strong motivation for attackers. Defenders must maintain security continuously, while attackers need to succeed only once.

Understanding this arms-race dynamic tempers expectations for achieving perfect security. Effective defense requires accepting that determined adversaries will eventually succeed. The goal becomes raising attack costs, detecting intrusions rapidly, and minimizing damage when breaches occur.

1.5 Toward Secure AI Systems

Defense in Depth

Securing AI systems requires layered defenses addressing multiple attack surfaces simultaneously. No single defensive technique provides comprehensive protection. Defense in depth acknowledges that some defenses will fail and ensures that subsequent layers contain damage.

Data Security forms the foundation. Provenance tracking documents data sources and transformations. Integrity verification detects corrupted data before it enters training. Access controls limit who can inject data into pipelines. Differential privacy adds noise to protect individual privacy. Anomaly detection identifies suspicious data patterns. Each mechanism addresses specific threats while complementing others.

Model Security hardens the AI artifacts themselves. Adversarial training exposes models to attack examples during development. Input validation rejects obviously adversarial queries. Output filtering detects and blocks suspicious predictions. Model watermarking enables the detection of intellectual property theft. Ensemble methods combine multiple models to improve robustness. Version control tracks model changes and enables rollback after compromise.

Infrastructure Security protects the computational environment. Secure enclaves isolate sensitive computations. Encrypted inference prevents eavesdropping on predictions. Authentication and authorization control access to model services. Rate limiting prevents resource exhaustion.

Monitoring systems detect anomalous query patterns or performance degradation.

Process Security embeds security throughout the development lifecycle. Threat modeling identifies potential attacks during the design phase. Security testing validates robustness before deployment. Incident response plans enable rapid reaction to breaches. Regular audits assess compliance with security policies. Continuous education keeps development teams up to date on emerging threats.

Layered defenses create multiple obstacles for adversaries. Breaching one layer triggers detection and response mechanisms. Complete compromise requires defeating all layers simultaneously, dramatically increasing the difficulty and cost of attacks.

Security-Aware Design

Building secure AI requires incorporating security considerations from the earliest design stages rather than adding security as an afterthought. Security-aware design makes fundamental architectural choices that minimize attack surfaces and enable effective defenses.

The Principle of Least Privilege dictates that systems should operate with the minimum necessary permissions. AI models should access only the data required for their specific function. Inference services should expose minimal information about model internals. This principle limits damage when components become compromised.

Fail-Safe Defaults ensure that security failures default to safe states. If authentication fails, deny access rather than permitting it. If input validation detects anomalies, reject the input rather than processing it. If model predictions seem suspicious, request human review rather than acting autonomously. These defaults prevent single points of failure from cascading into complete breaches.

Complete Mediation requires checking authorization on every access to protected resources. Models should not cache authorization decisions that might become stale. Each inference request should undergo fresh validation. This principle prevents time-of-check-time-of-use vulnerabilities.

Open Design recognizes that security through obscurity provides false confidence. Defensive mechanisms should remain effective even when adversaries understand them fully. Publishing defense details enables the security community to review and strengthen protections. However, specific deployment details, such as model architectures, may remain confidential to increase the cost to attackers.

Separation of Concerns divides functionality into components with minimal interdependencies. Training infrastructure should be separate from inference infrastructure. Data processing should be separate from model serving. This separation limits the impact of compromising individual components and simplifies security auditing.

The Mechanism's economy favors simple designs over complex ones. Complexity breeds vulnerabilities, as interactions between components can lead to unexpected behaviors. Simple, well-understood defensive mechanisms prove easier to implement correctly and validate thoroughly.

These principles provide guidance for security-conscious design choices throughout AI system development. Applying them consistently from project inception lays the foundation for robust security.

The Path Forward

AI security remains an evolving field. New attack vectors emerge as AI capabilities advance. Defensive techniques improve but never achieve perfect protection. Several key insights should guide future development:

Security Cannot Be Bolted On. Organizations must integrate security throughout the AI development lifecycle. Post-deployment hardening proves inadequate against sophisticated adversaries. Security awareness must permeate teams from data scientists through deployment engineers.

Interdisciplinary Collaboration Is Essential. Effective AI security requires expertise spanning machine learning, systems security, cryptography, formal verification, and domain knowledge. No single discipline provides complete answers. Success demands teams that communicate across traditional boundaries.

Transparency Builds Trust. Organizations should clearly communicate the capabilities, limitations, and failure modes of their AI systems. Transparency about security incidents enables industry-wide learning. Secret failures only help adversaries who independently discover the same vulnerabilities.

Regulatory Engagement Matters. As AI systems affect more aspects of society, regulation will increase. Organizations that engage constructively with regulators help shape sensible policies. Those that resist regulation risk onerous requirements developed without technical input.

Research Investment Pays Dividends. Many fundamental AI security questions remain open. How can we formally verify neural network properties? Can we achieve both privacy and utility in federated learning? How do we detect backdoors in pre-trained models? Answering these questions requires sustained research investment.

The following chapters build upon these foundations. We will examine specific attack vectors in detail, explore defensive techniques in depth, and provide practical guidance for implementing secure AI systems. The goal is not to present AI security as solved but to equip practitioners with tools and knowledge to address current threats while preparing for future challenges.

Chapter Summary

This chapter established foundational concepts necessary for understanding AI security:

Core Architectures: Modern AI relies on neural networks that learn patterns from data. Different architectures, such as feedforward networks, CNNs, RNNs, transformers, and GNNs, make different trade-offs that affect their security properties. Understanding these architectures illuminates why certain attacks succeed and how defenses must adapt.

Historical Evolution: AI progressed through symbolic reasoning, statistical learning, deep learning, and foundation model eras. Each wave introduced new capabilities and new vulnerabilities. Current security challenges reflect the accumulated complexity of all previous eras.

Development Lifecycle: AI systems move through data collection, curation, feature engineering, training, validation, deployment, and monitoring phases. Each phase exposes distinct attack surfaces. Comprehensive security requires addressing the entire lifecycle.

Fundamental Vulnerabilities: AI systems suffer from brittleness in high-dimensional spaces, opacity that prevents verification, data dependency that propagates corruption, and arms race dynamics that favor attackers. These fundamental properties demand new security paradigms.

Defensive Strategies: Security requires defense in depth with layered protections, security-aware design that incorporates protection from inception, and ongoing vigilance as threats evolve. No single technique provides complete protection.

Armed with these foundations, we proceed to examine specific threats and defenses in detail. The next chapter explores the adversarial attack landscape, providing concrete examples of how attackers exploit AI vulnerabilities and what these attacks reveal about AI system properties.

Key Takeaways

1. AI security differs fundamentally from traditional software security due to learned behavior, data dependency, and high-dimensional complexity.

2. Neural networks exhibit brittleness where imperceptible perturbations cause dramatic prediction changes, enabling adversarial examples.

3. Model opacity prevents verification and auditing while allowing backdoors to hide effectively in distributed representations.

4. Each phase of the AI development lifecycle introduces specific vulnerabilities that defenders must address systematically.

5. Effective AI security requires defense in depth, security-aware design principles, and acceptance that perfect security remains unattainable.

6. The AI security landscape evolves continuously as capabilities advance and adversaries adapt. Sustained research and interdisciplinary collaboration are essential.

Reflection Questions

1. How do the security challenges of AI systems deployed on edge devices differ from those in cloud environments?

2. If model opacity prevents formal verification, what alternative approaches can provide assurance about AI system behavior?

3. Consider an organization deploying a facial recognition system. What attack surfaces does the full development lifecycle expose?

4. How might the emergence of foundation models change the threat landscape compared to task-specific models?

5. What tensions exist between improving AI performance and ensuring security? Can these tensions be resolved or only managed?

2

The Adversarial Threat Landscape

Learning Objectives

By the end of this chapter, you will:

- Understand the primary attack vectors targeting AI systems across their lifecycle
- Recognize how adversarial examples exploit geometric properties of neural networks
- Identify data poisoning techniques and their long-term impacts on model behavior
- Comprehend privacy attacks that extract sensitive information from trained models
- Evaluate emerging threats unique to large language models and foundation models
- Apply threat modeling frameworks to assess organizational risk exposure

Introduction: Understanding the Adversary

The security of AI systems cannot be understood without examining the adversaries seeking to compromise them. Unlike traditional software, where attackers exploit implementation bugs, AI adversaries exploit fundamental properties of machine learning itself. They manipulate training data, craft inputs that trigger misclassification, extract proprietary models, and violate user privacy through inference attacks.

This chapter systematically explores the adversarial threat landscape. We examine each major attack category, analyze underlying mechanisms, and assess real-world implications. Understanding these threats provides essential context for the defensive strategies we will explore in subsequent chapters.

The adversarial landscape continues evolving as AI capabilities advance. Attacks that seemed theoretical five years ago now appear in production systems. Foundation models introduce entirely new vulnerability classes. Our treatment emphasizes both established threats and emerging risks that will shape future security challenges.

2.1 Adversarial Examples: Exploiting Decision Boundaries

The Fundamental Vulnerability

Adversarial examples represent one of the most surprising and concerning vulnerabilities in modern AI systems. These carefully crafted inputs cause models to confidently make incorrect predictions despite appearing identical to legitimate human inputs.

The vulnerability arises from the geometric properties of the high-dimensional spaces in which neural networks operate. Consider an image classifier processing 224x224 pixel color images. This creates a 150,528-dimensional space (224 × 224 × 3 color channels). In such high-dimensional spaces, decision boundaries separating different classes lie extremely close to typical data points. The average distance to the nearest decision boundary decreases as dimensionality increases.

Neural networks learn to partition this high-dimensional space based on training examples. During training, the network adjusts decision boundaries to correctly classify training data. However, the vast majority of the high-dimensional space remains unexplored during training. The density of training data becomes exponentially sparse as dimensionality increases.

This sparsity creates vulnerability. Adversaries can find directions in high-dimensional space that cross decision boundaries while remaining imperceptible to humans. The mathematical structure of neural networks makes such directions abundant and relatively easy to compute.

Attack Mechanisms

Several methods exist for generating adversarial examples, each with different capabilities and requirements:

Gradient-Based Attacks leverage the fact that neural networks are differentiable functions. Attackers compute gradients that indicate how to modify inputs to maximize classification error. The Fast Gradient Sign Method (FGSM) takes a single step in the direction of the gradient. More sophisticated variants, such as Projected Gradient Descent (PGD), take multiple smaller steps while constraining the perturbation magnitude.

These attacks prove remarkably effective. Adding noise with a magnitude equivalent to changing a single pixel value by less than one percent can flip classifications with high reliability. The perturbations remain imperceptible when viewing images normally but dramatically alter model predictions.

Optimization-Based Attacks formulate adversarial example generation as an optimization problem. The Carlini-Wagner attack minimizes perturbation size while ensuring misclassification. This approach generates more subtle perturbations than gradient-based methods but requires more computation.

Optimization-based attacks can target specific misclassifications. An attacker might want to ensure a stop sign gets classified as a speed limit sign rather than just any incorrect class. The optimization objective encodes this preference, producing targeted adversarial examples.

Black-Box Attacks operate without access to model gradients or parameters. Attackers treat models as black boxes that accept inputs and return predictions. Query-based attacks submit many inputs and analyze outputs to infer the decision boundary structure. Transfer-based attacks generate adversarial examples for surrogate models and rely on those examples transferring to the target model.

Transfer attacks prove surprisingly effective. Adversarial examples crafted for one model frequently fool different models, even those with different architectures. This property enables attackers to develop attacks offline against publicly available models before targeting proprietary production systems.

Physical-World Attacks extend adversarial examples beyond digital perturbations. Attackers create physical objects or patterns that reliably fool vision systems. Adversarial patches represent self-contained patterns that cause misclassification when placed in an image. Researchers demonstrated stop signs with stickers that autonomous vehicle vision systems classify as speed limit signs.

Physical attacks must overcome additional challenges. Camera distortions, lighting variations, and viewing angles affect appearance. Robust physical attacks exploit expectations over transformations during generation, producing perturbations that remain effective across diverse conditions.

Attack Scenarios and Implications

Adversarial examples threaten numerous real-world systems:

Autonomous Vehicles rely on computer vision for navigation and obstacle detection. Adversarial attacks could cause vehicles to misidentify traffic signs, fail to detect pedestrians, or misinterpret road markings. The physical nature of autonomous driving enables the creation of adversarial patches and patterns on real objects.

Facial Recognition systems used for authentication face adversarial threats from both digital and physical attacks. Attackers might add imperceptible perturbations to photos to evade identification. Adversarial glasses and makeup patterns demonstrated in research could enable impersonation or evasion in physical settings.

Malware Detection systems using machine learning prove vulnerable to adversarial examples. Attackers add benign-seeming code that preserves malicious functionality while evading detection. The discrete nature of programs complicates but does not prevent adversarial attacks on malware classifiers.

Content Moderation systems filtering harmful content face adversarial manipulation. Small text modifications might render hate speech undetectable. Image perturbations could allow prohibited content to bypass filters. The arms race between platforms and adversaries continues escalating.

Medical Diagnosis systems analyzing medical imagery could be compromised through adversarial examples. Subtle perturbations in CT scans or X-rays might hide tumors or lead to false positives. The life-critical nature of medical AI makes adversarial robustness essential.

The Transferability Problem

Adversarial examples exhibit remarkable transferability across models. An adversarial example crafted for Model A frequently fools Model B, even if the models have different architectures, training procedures, or datasets. This property has profound security implications.

Transferability arises because different models learn similar decision boundaries when trained on related tasks. Although the exact boundary locations differ, the general structure exhibits similarities. Adversarial examples that cross boundaries in one model often cross corresponding boundaries in other models.

Several factors influence transferability:

Architecture Similarity affects transfer rates. Adversarial examples transfer more reliably between models with similar architectures. However, transfer occurs even across fundamentally different architectures, such as CNNs and Vision Transformers.

Training Data Overlap increases transferability. Models trained on similar datasets learn more similar representations. However, transfer succeeds even with limited data overlap, suggesting the vulnerability stems from fundamental properties of neural network training.

Attack Strength correlates with transferability. Stronger perturbations that move farther from decision boundaries tend to transfer more reliably. However, even minimal perturbations exhibit non-trivial transfer rates.

Transferability enables black-box attacks against proprietary models. Attackers train surrogate models on similar data, generate adversarial examples for the surrogates, and deploy those examples against target systems. This strategy requires no access to target model internals.

2.2 Data Poisoning: Corrupting the Learning Process

The Supply Chain Attack

Data poisoning attacks compromise AI systems by corrupting training data. Unlike adversarial examples that target deployed models, poisoning attacks occur during development. Poisoned training data causes models to learn incorrect patterns that persist throughout their operational lifetime.

The attack is particularly insidious because it occurs before deployment. Organizations may extensively test models before production release. However, testing typically validates performance on clean data. Poisoned models may perform normally on most inputs while harboring backdoors that activate under specific conditions.

Data poisoning exploits the fundamental dependence of machine learning on the quality of training data. Models learn exclusively from examples provided during training. If those examples systematically misrepresent reality, the model incorporates those misrepresentations into its learned function.

Poisoning Attack Categories

Availability Attacks degrade overall model performance by injecting corrupted examples. The goal is to reduce model accuracy across all inputs rather than targeting specific behaviors. Availability attacks might reduce spam filter effectiveness, diminish fraud detection capabilities, or impair the accuracy of medical diagnoses.

Random label flipping provides a simple availability attack. Attackers flip training labels on a fraction of examples. Even small poisoning fractions significantly degrade model performance. A 10 percent label flip rate can reduce accuracy by 20-30 percent in many applications.

Targeted Attacks create specific model behaviors while maintaining normal performance on most inputs. The attacker wants a spam filter to misclassify specific emails as legitimate while still catching other spam. Or a facial recognition system should misidentify a particular individual while correctly identifying others.

Clean-label poisoning demonstrates the sophistication of targeted attacks. The attacker modifies training examples without changing their labels. A correctly labeled cat image receives subtle modifications that create a hidden association between the modification pattern and the cat class.

After training, test images with the modification pattern get classified as cats regardless of actual content.

Backdoor Attacks embed triggers that activate malicious behavior. The model performs normally on standard inputs but behaves incorrectly when inputs contain specific trigger patterns. Backdoor attacks prove extremely difficult to detect because they maintain high accuracy on clean test data.

Physical backdoor triggers enable real-world attacks. A traffic sign classifier might contain a backdoor triggered by a specific sticker pattern. Stop signs with that pattern get misclassified as speed limit signs. The backdoor remains dormant until the attacker deploys the physical trigger in the environment.

Poisoning Mechanisms

Direct Training Data Corruption occurs when attackers compromise data collection infrastructure. Web scraping bots poisoned at the source collect corrupted data. Compromised sensors inject poisoned samples. Insider threats provide the most direct path to corrupting training data.

Crowdsourcing Attacks exploit human annotation processes. Attackers create accounts on crowdsourcing platforms and submit malicious labels. Quality control mechanisms struggle to detect sophisticated poisoning where labels appear plausible.

Data Augmentation Exploitation leverages automated data expansion. Many training pipelines augment datasets by applying transformations like rotation, scaling, or color adjustment. Attackers craft poison samples that amplify through augmentation, multiplying their impact.

Transfer Learning Poisoning compromises the foundations of foundation models used for downstream tasks. Organizations increasingly fine-tune pre-trained models rather than training from scratch. Poisoned foundation models propagate vulnerabilities to all downstream applications.

Federated Learning Attacks target distributed training scenarios. Malicious participants in federated learning submit poisoned model updates. Aggregation mechanisms struggle to distinguish malicious from benign updates, especially when multiple participants collude.

Detection and Defense Challenges

Detecting poisoned training data proves extremely difficult:

Scale Challenges arise from massive training datasets. Modern AI systems train on millions or billions of examples. Manually auditing such datasets for subtle corruptions remains infeasible.

Imperceptibility means poisoned samples may appear legitimate. Clean-label attacks modify examples without changing labels. Backdoor triggers can be subtle patterns difficult to detect through visual inspection.

Statistical Similarity allows poisoned samples to match the distribution properties of clean data. Attackers craft poison that remains statistically indistinguishable from legitimate examples when analyzed at the aggregate level.

Testing Limitations mean standard validation fails to reveal poisoning. Models maintain high accuracy on clean test sets while harboring backdoors. Specialized testing to target backdoor detection is necessary.

Defense requires multilayered approaches addressing different attack phases. Data provenance tracking documents example sources. Anomaly detection identifies statistical outliers. Robust learning algorithms tolerate limited poisoning. Testing specifically probes for backdoor behaviors. However, no single technique provides complete protection.

2.3 Model Extraction: Intellectual Property Theft

The Attack Vector

Model extraction attacks steal intellectual property by replicating AI model functionality through systematic querying. Organizations invest significant resources in developing proprietary models. Attackers seek to replicate these capabilities without incurring development costs.

The attack exploits the model-as-a-service paradigm. Organizations monetize AI by exposing model capabilities through APIs. Users submit queries and receive predictions without accessing model internals. However, attackers can query models systematically to infer their behavior.

Model extraction proves particularly concerning because it enables follow-on attacks. Once attackers possess functionally equivalent models, they can generate adversarial examples offline. They can analyze model vulnerabilities without detection. They can fine-tune extracted models for malicious purposes.

Extraction Techniques

Query-Based Extraction submits carefully chosen inputs and analyzes outputs to reconstruct model behavior. The attacker treats the target model as a black box that accepts queries and returns predictions. Strategic query selection maximizes information gained per query.

Active learning strategies guide query selection. The attacker maintains a surrogate model that approximates target behavior. Queries target regions where the surrogate model remains uncertain, maximizing information gain. This approach efficiently explores the structure of the decision boundary.

The number of queries required depends on the model's complexity and the desired fidelity. Simple linear models can be extracted with queries equal to the number of parameters. Deep neural networks require more queries, but practical attacks succeed with tens of thousands of queries for many applications.

Equation-Solving Attacks directly compute model parameters for certain architectures. Linear models and simple neural networks can be represented as systems of equations. Solving these systems reveals exact parameter values. This approach works for models with relatively few parameters but becomes intractable for large networks.

Architecture Reconstruction attempts to infer the target model's structure. Attackers analyze prediction characteristics like output dimensions, confidence patterns, and timing information. This information constrains possible architectures. Combining architecture knowledge with query-based extraction improves attack efficiency.

Prediction API Abuse exploits overly informative API responses. Some services return not only class predictions but also confidence scores for all classes. This detailed information dramatically accelerates extraction. Defenders must balance the informativeness of APIs against extraction risk.

High-Value Targets

Several domains face particular model extraction risks:

Large Language Models represent massive investments in compute and data. Their capabilities can be partially extracted through systematic prompting. Attackers generate synthetic training data by querying the model and training substitute models on the responses.

Recommendation Systems contain valuable business logic about user preferences and item relationships. Extraction attacks create competing services without developing original recommendation algorithms.

Fraud Detection Models protect financial systems. Extracted models reveal exactly which behaviors trigger fraud alerts, enabling adversaries to craft fraud that evades detection.

Medical Diagnosis Systems embody expensive medical expertise. Extraction enables competitors to replicate capabilities without investing in model development or data collection.

Autonomous Vehicle Models contain sophisticated perception and planning algorithms. Extraction accelerates competitor development while potentially revealing exploitable vulnerabilities.

Economic and Security Implications

Model extraction creates both economic and security harms:

Intellectual Property Loss undermines the business model for AI-as-a-service providers. If models can be easily extracted, customers have an incentive to extract rather than subscribe. This threatens the economic viability of prediction service businesses.

Competitive Disadvantage occurs when competitors extract models rather than innovate independently. Organizations that invest in AI development lose their competitive advantage to free riders.

Adversarial Attack Enablement represents the primary security concern. Extracted models enable attackers to generate adversarial examples and discover vulnerabilities offline without alerting defenders.

Cascading Risks occur when extracted models themselves become targets. An extracted model might be less secure than the original, creating weaknesses that propagate through the ecosystem.

2.4 Privacy Attacks: Extracting Sensitive Information

Privacy Vulnerabilities in Machine Learning

Machine learning models memorize information from their training data. This memorization enables generalization but creates privacy risks.

Careful querying can extract information about training data, potentially revealing sensitive personal information.

Privacy attacks exploit the fundamental tension between model utility and data privacy. Useful models must capture patterns from training data. However, capturing too much detail about individual training examples violates privacy.

Attack Categories

Membership Inference Attacks determine whether a specific example appeared in the model's training set. The attacker has a data point and wants to know whether it was used for training. Successful inference violates privacy by revealing information about the dataset composition.

The attack leverages overfitting tendencies. Models typically achieve higher confidence on training examples than on new data. By measuring prediction confidence, attackers can infer membership with success rates significantly above random guessing.

Membership inference proves particularly concerning for sensitive applications. Consider a model trained on medical records. Successfully inferring that a particular patient's records appeared in the training set reveals that they have the condition being modeled. This inference alone constitutes a privacy violation.

Attribute Inference Attacks infer sensitive attributes about individuals from model predictions. Even if the model wasn't explicitly trained to predict the sensitive attribute, correlations in the training data can still enable inference.

For example, a model predicting loan default risk might reveal information about an applicant's race or health status by correlating with observable features. The model learned these correlations from the training data without the sensitive attributes being explicitly labeled.

Model Inversion Attacks reconstruct training data from model parameters or predictions. Early work demonstrated the reconstruction of facial images from face recognition model parameters. More recent attacks extract training examples from generative models and language models.

Language models prove particularly vulnerable to model inversion. These models sometimes memorize and regurgitate verbatim text from training documents. Attackers can extract personal information, private communications, and confidential documents through carefully crafted prompts.

Training Data Extraction from large language models represents an emerging and serious privacy threat. Researchers demonstrated the extraction of memorized training examples, including names, phone numbers, email addresses, and even verbatim copyrighted text. The scale of language model training data makes auditing memorization infeasible.

Privacy Risk Factors

Several factors influence privacy attack success:

Overfitting increases privacy risk. Models that memorize training data rather than learning general patterns prove more vulnerable. Regularization techniques that prevent overfitting also provide some privacy protection.

Model Capacity affects memorization. Larger models with excess capacity memorize more training details. The trend toward ever-larger models exacerbates privacy concerns.

Training Data Duplication amplifies memorization. Examples that appear multiple times in the training data are memorized more reliably. Deduplication provides simple but important privacy protection.

Sensitive Information Prevalence in training data determines attack impact. Datasets with abundant personally identifiable information create greater privacy risks than those with sanitized data.

Query Access enables privacy attacks. Unrestricted model access allows adversaries to submit carefully crafted queries that extract information. Rate limiting and query monitoring mitigate some attack vectors.

Real-World Privacy Concerns

Privacy attacks threaten various domains:

Healthcare AI systems train on sensitive patient data. Privacy violations could reveal medical conditions, treatment histories, or genetic information. Regulatory frameworks like HIPAA make such violations legally actionable.

Financial Services models train on transaction data and credit histories. Privacy breaches may expose information about individuals' financial situations, spending patterns, or creditworthiness.

Social Media platforms train models on user communications and behavior. Privacy attacks could extract private messages, reveal social connections, or expose behavioral patterns users intended to keep private.

Surveillance Systems using facial recognition train on images of individuals. Model inversion attacks might reconstruct faces of people in the training set, revealing who was surveilled.

Enterprise AI systems train on confidential business data. Privacy attacks could extract trade secrets, strategic plans, or competitive intelligence.

2.5 Integrity and Availability Attacks

Compromising Model Reliability

Beyond confidentiality violations, adversaries target model integrity and availability. These attacks aim to corrupt model behavior or deny service to legitimate users.

Model Manipulation Attacks directly modify model parameters or architecture. If attackers gain access to stored models, they can alter parameters to induce desired behaviors. Weight manipulation attacks inject vulnerabilities while maintaining acceptable performance on test data.

Such attacks prove particularly concerning in supply chain contexts. Pre-trained models from untrusted sources might contain hidden manipulations. Organizations that download and fine-tune public models face risks from backdoors embedded in the initial weights.

Byzantine Attacks target federated learning scenarios where multiple parties collaboratively train models. Malicious participants submit corrupted model updates designed to degrade or compromise the global model. Byzantine fault tolerance becomes crucial but faces scalability challenges.

Gradient Manipulation in distributed training corrupts the learning process by providing false gradient information. Attackers participating in distributed training compute and submit incorrect gradients that steer model convergence toward desired behaviors.

Availability Attacks

Denial-of-Service attacks overwhelm the model-serving infrastructure. Adversaries submit floods of queries that exhaust computational resources. Unlike traditional DDoS attacks that target network bandwidth, AI-specific DoS attacks exploit computational bottlenecks.

Adversarial Sponge Examples represent a sophisticated availability attack. These carefully crafted inputs trigger worst-case computational complexity in neural network inference. Processing sponge examples consumes far more resources than typical inputs.

Model Staleness Attacks exploit continuous learning systems. Adversaries submit inputs that corrupt online learning mechanisms, causing models to degrade over time. The gradual nature makes detection difficult.

Resource Exhaustion through expensive queries targets systems with variable computational costs. Attackers identify queries that maximize processing time while appearing legitimate. Video analysis, complex reasoning tasks, and extensive language generation provide attack opportunities.

2.6 Emerging Threats

Foundation Model Vulnerabilities

Large language models and other foundation models introduce novel attack vectors:

Prompt Injection Attacks manipulate models by embedding instructions in inputs. Unlike SQL injection, which exploits parsing vulnerabilities, prompt injection exploits the models' training to follow instructions. Attackers craft prompts that override system instructions or extract sensitive information.

Jailbreaking attempts bypass safety measures in language models. Developers implement guardrails preventing models from generating harmful content. Jailbreaks use carefully crafted prompts to circumvent these protections. The arms race between developers adding restrictions and attackers finding bypasses continues escalating.

Data Extraction from foundation models proves easier than from smaller models. The massive amount of training data and the model's capacity increase memorization. Attackers extract training examples including copyrighted text, personal information, and confidential documents.

Model Repurposing leverages openly available foundation models for malicious purposes. Fine-tuning language models on harmful data creates tools for generating misinformation, phishing content, or malicious code. The democratization of powerful AI capabilities empowers both beneficial and harmful applications.

Multimodal Attack Vectors

Systems processing multiple data types (text, images, audio) face unique threats:

Cross-Modal Adversarial Examples exploit systems that combine different modalities. An image-text model might be fooled by adversarial images that misalign with the accompanying text. Attackers exploit the integration of multiple neural networks processing different modalities.

Modality Confusion Attacks cause models to misinterpret which modality carries primary information. An image with embedded text might be processed as text rather than as imagery, or vice versa, leading to incorrect handling.

Synchronization Attacks target temporal alignment in multimodal systems. Audio-visual models might be confused by desynchronization between modalities. Deepfake detection systems prove particularly vulnerable to such attacks.

Automated Attack Generation

AI increasingly enables sophisticated attacks against AI systems:

Adversarial Example Automation uses neural networks to generate adversarial perturbations more efficiently than traditional optimization methods. Generative models can quickly learn to produce adversarial examples without per-example optimization.

Poisoning Attack Optimization employs machine learning to craft maximally effective poison samples. Attackers train meta-models that optimize poisoning strategies across multiple scenarios.

Attack Transfer Enhancement uses machine learning to improve the transferability of adversarial examples. Models learn to generate perturbations that transfer more reliably across different target systems.

2.7 Real-World Attack Case Studies

Case Study 1: Adversarial Stop Signs

Researchers demonstrated physical adversarial attacks against traffic sign classifiers. They created stop signs with carefully placed stickers that caused autonomous vehicle vision systems to misclassify them as speed limit signs. The attack succeeded consistently across different viewing angles and lighting conditions.

The research highlighted several key lessons. Physical-world attacks face additional constraints but remain viable. Robustness testing must include physical adversarial examples, not just digital perturbations. Safety-critical AI systems require defenses against adversarial attacks before deployment.

Case Study 2: Poisoned ImageNet

Security researchers successfully poisoned a widely used image classification dataset. They submitted corrupted images to open-source datasets that many organizations used for training. Models trained on the poisoned data contained backdoors that triggered on specific patterns.

This case demonstrated supply chain vulnerabilities in AI development. Organizations trusting public datasets faced risks from poisoned examples. The incident catalyzed the development of data-provenance tracking and poisoning-detection techniques.

Case Study 3: Language Model Data Extraction

Academic researchers extracted memorized training examples from large language models. They successfully extracted names, phone numbers, addresses, and verbatim passages from books and articles. Some extracted content included personally identifiable information never intended for public release.

The research revealed serious privacy implications of training on web-scraped data. It demonstrated that common privacy protections, such as deduplication, are insufficient. The findings prompted reevaluation of training data curation practices across the industry.

Case Study 4: Model Extraction from Prediction APIs

Security researchers demonstrated a practical model extraction against commercial prediction APIs. They systematically queried services and trained substitute models, achieving performance equivalent to that of the original services. The attacks required only thousands of queries, well within typical API rate limits.

The case revealed weaknesses in protecting AI intellectual property. It showed that rate limiting alone provides insufficient protection. Defensive techniques like watermarking and query pattern analysis became priorities for service providers.

Case Study 5: Membership Inference Against Medical ML

Researchers successfully performed membership inference attacks against models trained on medical datasets. They determined which patients' records were present in the training data with significantly higher accuracy than random guessing. This constituted a serious privacy violation under healthcare regulations.

The case demonstrated that privacy risks from machine learning extend beyond data breaches. Model access alone enables privacy attacks. It motivated the adoption of differential privacy and federated learning in healthcare AI applications.

Chapter Summary

This chapter explored the adversarial threat landscape facing AI systems:

Adversarial Examples: Neural networks prove vulnerable to imperceptible perturbations that cause misclassification. These attacks exploit high-dimensional geometry and exhibit surprising transferability across models. Both digital and physical attacks threaten real-world systems.

Data Poisoning: Corrupting training data creates persistent vulnerabilities that survive into deployment. Poisoning attacks range from availability attacks that degrade overall performance to sophisticated backdoors activated by specific triggers.

Model Extraction: Systematic querying enables attackers to replicate the functionality of proprietary models. Extraction threatens AI-as-a-service business models and enables follow-on attacks against the original systems.

Privacy Attacks: Models memorize training data, enabling membership inference, attribute inference, and data reconstruction attacks. Privacy violations are particularly concerning in sensitive applications such as healthcare, finance, and surveillance.

Integrity and Availability: Direct manipulation attacks compromise model parameters while maintaining superficial correctness. Availability attacks exhaust computational resources through adversarial queries.

Emerging Threats: Foundation models face prompt injection, jailbreaking, and enhanced data extraction risks. Multimodal systems introduce cross-modal attack vectors. AI-powered attacks increasingly automate the generation of adversarial examples and the deployment of poisoning strategies.

Understanding these threats provides essential context for the defensive strategies we will explore in subsequent chapters. No single defense addresses all attack vectors. Effective security requires layered protections informed by comprehensive threat modeling.

Key Takeaways

1. Adversarial examples exploit fundamental geometric properties of high-dimensional decision boundaries, not implementation bugs. This makes them difficult to eliminate completely.

2. Data poisoning attacks occur before deployment, creating persistent vulnerabilities that standard testing fails to detect. Supply chain security becomes critical.

3. Model extraction enables intellectual property theft and facilitates follow-on attacks. API design must balance utility against extraction risk.

4. Privacy attacks extract sensitive information from models even when the information wasn't explicitly included in outputs. Memorization creates fundamental tensions with utility.

5. Emerging threats from foundation models and automated attack generation continue expanding the adversarial landscape. Defensive strategies must evolve continuously.

6. Real-world case studies demonstrate that theoretical attacks translate into practical vulnerabilities. Security cannot rely on attackers lacking motivation or capability.

Reflection Questions

1. Consider an organization deploying a facial recognition system for building access control. What attack vectors pose the greatest risk, and how would you prioritize defenses?

2. How does the transferability of adversarial examples change the threat model compared to attacks that require white-box access to target models?

3. If data poisoning occurs during training but manifests as a deployment vulnerability, what organizational processes could detect the problem before production release?

4. What tensions exist between protecting model intellectual property through restricted APIs and providing useful service to legitimate users? Can these tensions be resolved?

5. As foundation models become more capable, how might the nature of adversarial threats evolve? What attack vectors that seem infeasible today might become practical?

6. Compare the relative difficulty of defending against adversarial examples (inference-time attacks) versus data poisoning.

3

Developing Secure AI Systems

Learning Objectives

By the end of this chapter, you will:

- Apply security-by-design principles throughout the AI development lifecycle
- Implement secure data collection, curation, and preparation practices
- Develop threat models specific to AI system architectures
- Establish secure training procedures that resist poisoning attacks
- Design validation frameworks that test for security properties
- Create deployment architectures that minimize attack surfaces
- Build monitoring systems that detect anomalous model behavior

Introduction: Shifting Left on Security

Traditional software development often treats security as a post-development concern. Developers build features first, and security teams harden systems before deployment. This approach proves inadequate for AI systems in which security vulnerabilities can be embedded during training and persist throughout their operational lifetimes.

Secure AI development requires shifting security left in the development lifecycle. Security considerations must inform every decision from initial data collection through deployment and maintenance. This chapter provides a comprehensive framework for building security into AI systems from inception.

We organize our discussion around the AI development lifecycle. Each phase introduces specific security challenges requiring tailored defensive strategies. We emphasize practical implementation guidance over abstract principles, providing actionable recommendations that development teams can apply immediately.

The framework presented here assumes adversarial environments where determined attackers seek to compromise systems. While not all deployments face such threats, designing for adversarial scenarios creates robust systems that gracefully handle benign failures.

3.1 Security-by-Design Principles

Core Security Principles

Several fundamental security principles guide secure AI development:

Defense in Depth recognizes that no single security mechanism provides complete protection. Multiple independent defensive layers ensure that breaching one mechanism does not compromise the entire system. For AI systems, defense in depth spans data validation, model hardening, infrastructure security, and monitoring systems.

Each layer operates independently, detecting and preventing different attack vectors. Data validation catches poisoned training examples before they enter the pipeline. Adversarial training hardens models against evasion attacks. Infrastructure controls prevent unauthorized model access. Monitoring systems detect anomalous behavior during deployment. Attackers must defeat all layers to achieve their objectives.

Least Privilege limits access rights to the minimum necessary for each system component. Training processes should not have access to the production database. Inference services should not have access to training data. Human operators should not have unrestricted access to model parameters. Enforcing least privilege can cause damage when components are compromised.

For AI systems, least privilege extends beyond traditional access control. Models should have access only to the features necessary for their task. Inference APIs should return minimal information enabling predictions without revealing model internals. Training pipelines should process data with minimal retention after use.

Fail-Safe Defaults ensure that security failures default to safe states rather than permissive ones. Authentication failures should deny access. Input validation failures should reject inputs. Anomaly detection uncertainties should trigger alerts. This principle prevents single points of failure from cascading into complete breaches.

AI systems should implement fail-safe defaults at multiple levels. If training data validation detects anomalies, halt training rather than continuing with suspicious data. If deployed models exhibit unexpected behavior, route requests to human review rather than acting autonomously. If monitoring systems lose visibility, assume compromise rather than continued normal operation.

Complete Mediation requires security checks on every access to protected resources. Systems should not cache authorization decisions that might become stale. Each inference request should undergo fresh authentication and input validation. Each training run should verify data provenance. Bypassing these checks creates vulnerabilities that adversaries can exploit.

The Mechanism's economy favors simple security mechanisms over complex ones. Complexity breeds vulnerabilities, as component interactions can lead to unexpected behaviors. Simple, well-understood mechanisms prove easier to implement correctly, audit thoroughly, and maintain over time.

This principle is particularly important for AI systems, where model complexity already challenges understanding. Security mechanisms should add minimal complexity. Prefer straightforward input validation over complex parsing. Use simple access control models over elaborate permission systems. Choose transparent monitoring over opaque anomaly detection.

Separation of Privilege requires multiple conditions for sensitive operations. No single compromised component should enable a complete system breach. Critical operations, such as model deployment, require approval from multiple parties. Sensitive data access requires both authentication and authorization. This principle makes attacks more difficult by requiring adversaries to compromise multiple independent systems.

Threat Modeling for AI Systems

Threat modeling systematically identifies potential attacks and guides defensive priorities. AI systems require specialized threat modeling that accounts for machine learning vulnerabilities beyond traditional software threats.

Asset Identification catalogs what needs protection. AI system assets include:

- Training data containing sensitive information or valuable intellectual property
- Trained models representing significant development investment
- Model predictions that inform critical decisions
- Infrastructure hosting training and inference workloads
- Training procedures and hyperparameters constituting proprietary knowledge

Each asset has different sensitivity levels and faces different threats. Training data might be more sensitive than model parameters. Model predictions might warrant more protection than training procedures. Threat modeling must assess each asset independently.

Threat Enumeration identifies potential attackers and their capabilities. AI systems face threats from multiple adversaries:

- External attackers seeking to steal intellectual property or compromise system integrity
- Malicious insiders with privileged access to data or models
- Careless users who inadvertently introduce vulnerabilities
- Compromised supply chain partners providing corrupted data or models
- Automated attacks leveraging other AI systems against targets

Each adversary type has different capabilities and motivations. External attackers typically operate through public interfaces. Insiders might have direct system access. Supply chain compromises introduce vulnerabilities before organizations take custody. Understanding adversary capabilities guides defensive priorities.

Attack Vector Analysis examines how threats might materialize. For AI systems, attack vectors include:

- Data poisoning through compromised collection infrastructure
- Adversarial examples submitted during inference
- Model extraction through systematic querying
- Privacy attacks inferring training data properties
- Backdoor injection during training or through pre-trained models
- Infrastructure compromise enabling parameter manipulation

Each attack vector requires different defensive measures. Data poisoning defenses focus on input validation and anomaly detection. Adversarial example defenses harden model decision boundaries. Extraction defenses limit query patterns and obfuscate responses. Comprehensive protection requires addressing all relevant vectors.

Risk Assessment prioritizes threats based on likelihood and impact. Not all threats warrant the same level of defensive investment. High-likelihood, high-impact threats demand immediate attention. Low-likelihood, low-impact threats might be accepted as residual risk.

For AI systems, risk assessment must consider both technical and business factors. A privacy attack might carry lower technical severity but higher regulatory and reputational impact. Model extraction might seem low-impact, but it enables follow-on attacks with severe consequences. Risk assessment requires collaboration between technical teams and business stakeholders.

Mitigation Strategy Development defines defenses against prioritized threats. Effective strategies employ multiple defensive layers addressing different attack phases. For data poisoning, strategies might combine:

- Provenance tracking documenting data sources
- Statistical validation detecting distributional anomalies
- Redundant annotation identifying label inconsistencies
- Robust training algorithms tolerating limited corruption
- Behavioral testing reveals backdoors in trained models

No single technique provides complete protection. Layered defenses ensure that failures in one mechanism do not lead to complete compromise.

Security Architecture Patterns

Several architectural patterns enhance AI system security:

Isolation Boundaries separate components with different security requirements. Training infrastructure should be isolated from production serving infrastructure. Data processing should occur in separate environments from model development. Credential management should be isolated from application logic.

Isolation limits damage from compromised components. If training infrastructure becomes compromised, attackers gain no direct access to production systems. If the serving infrastructure is compromised, attackers cannot directly manipulate the training data. Clear isolation boundaries simplify security auditing and incident response.

Zero Trust Architecture treats every request as potentially malicious regardless of origin. Systems verify identity and authorization for each operation rather than implicitly trusting authenticated users or network locations. For AI systems, zero trust means:

- Authenticating and authorizing every API request
- Validating every input before processing
- Encrypting all communication channels
- Logging all access for audit purposes
- Assuming breach and monitoring for compromise indicators

Zero trust proves particularly important for AI systems because attacks can originate from authenticated users or internal systems. Compromised accounts or insider threats require defenses beyond perimeter security.

API Gateway Pattern centralizes security enforcement for inference services. All requests are routed through a gateway that implements authentication, authorization, rate limiting, input validation, and logging. This pattern provides consistent security controls across multiple models and simplifies policy updates.

Gateway architectures enable sophisticated defensive techniques. Request throttling prevents extraction attacks. Input sanitization blocks adversarial examples. Response filtering prevents information leakage. Traffic analysis detects attack patterns. Centralizing these controls reduces implementation complexity and ensures consistent application.

Microservices with Security Boundaries decompose systems into small, independently deployable components with explicit security boundaries. Each microservice operates with minimal privileges and communicates through authenticated, authorized channels. This architecture limits the blast radius when components become compromised.

For AI systems, microservices might separate data ingestion, preprocessing, training, validation, deployment, and monitoring. Each service operates with access only to resources necessary for its function. Compromising data ingestion does not provide direct access to production models. Compromising inference services does not expose training data.

3.2 Secure Data Management

Data Collection Security

Secure data collection forms the foundation of secure AI systems. Compromised data sources produce compromised models regardless of downstream security measures.

Provenance Tracking documents the origins and transformations of data throughout the collection process. Each data point should carry metadata recording:

- Source system or sensor
- Collection timestamp
- Collection methodology
- Responsible party or process
- Any transformations applied
- Validation checks performed

Provenance enables auditing suspicious data patterns and tracing compromises back to their source. When poisoning attacks are detected, provenance information identifies affected data batches, enabling targeted remediation rather than complete retraining.

Source Authentication verifies that data originates from legitimate sources. Collection systems should authenticate data providers using strong cryptographic mechanisms. Digital signatures prove data authenticity and enable detecting tampering during transmission.

For crowdsourced data, authentication might combine cryptographic identity with reputation systems. Contributors with a history of high-quality submissions earn trust. New or low-reputation contributors face additional scrutiny. This approach balances open participation with resistance to poisoning.

Integrity Verification ensures data remains unmodified during collection and storage. Cryptographic hashes computed at collection time should match hashes at use time. Blockchain-based systems can provide immutable audit trails for high-value datasets.

Integrity verification must operate at appropriate granularity. Per-record hashes enable the detection of individual corrupted samples. Dataset-level hashes verify entire collection integrity. Both granularities provide complementary protection.

Secure Transmission protects data as it moves from collection points to storage. Transport Layer Security (TLS) encrypts network communications, preventing eavesdropping and tampering. Certificate pinning ensures connections to legitimate servers rather than man-in-the-middle attackers.

For high-sensitivity applications, end-to-end encryption protects data even from infrastructure providers. Data remains encrypted throughout transmission and storage, decrypting only during authorized processing. This approach proves essential for medical records, financial data, and other regulated information.

Data Curation and Preparation

Anomaly Detection identifies suspicious patterns in collected data. Statistical techniques detect distributional shifts that might indicate poisoning. Clustering algorithms identify outliers warranting investigation. Supervised methods flag samples inconsistent with known patterns.

Anomaly detection faces the challenge of distinguishing malicious corruption from benign noise. Natural data contains outliers representing unusual but legitimate examples. Effective detection requires domain expertise to interpret statistical signals and investigate suspicious cases.

Sanitization and filtering remove or correct problematic data. Personally identifiable information should be redacted or anonymized. Duplicates should be removed to prevent memorization. Irrelevant features should be filtered to reduce attack surfaces.

Sanitization requires careful balance. Over-aggressive filtering might remove important information, thereby reducing the model's utility. Under-sanitization leaves privacy and security vulnerabilities. Clear policies defining what constitutes sensitive information guide sanitization decisions.

Label Validation verifies the correctness of annotations in supervised learning. Multiple annotators should label subsets of data with disagreement, triggering review. Expert validation should sample annotations regularly. Automated consistency checks should identify obvious label errors.

For high-stakes applications, professional annotation services with rigorous quality control prove worthwhile. Crowdsourcing provides cost-effective scaling but requires robust validation to prevent poisoning through malicious or careless annotators.

Data Augmentation Security ensures that synthetic data generation does not introduce vulnerabilities. Augmentation transforms like rotation, scaling, and color adjustment should preserve semantic content. Augmentation should not amplify poisoned samples or create patterns that become backdoor triggers.

Testing augmentation pipelines with known poisoned samples verifies they do not amplify attacks. Regular audits of augmented data detect unexpected patterns. Limiting augmentation diversity prevents adversarial samples from being normalized by repeated transformations.

Data Storage and Access Control

Encryption at Rest protects stored data from unauthorized access. Industry-standard encryption algorithms, such as AES-256, should protect training datasets, models, and logs. Encryption keys should be managed through dedicated key management services with strict access controls.

Encryption provides defense in depth. If attackers compromise storage systems, they cannot read encrypted data without also compromising key management. In multi-tenant environments, per-tenant encryption keys provide customer isolation.

Access Control Policies limit data access to authorized personnel and systems. Role-based access control (RBAC) assigns permissions based on job functions. Attribute-based access control (ABAC) makes access decisions based on context, like data sensitivity and user clearance.

AI systems require granular access control. Data scientists might access development data but not production user data. Training systems might read training data but not write to production databases. Inference services might access models but not training data. Properly scoped permissions prevent privilege escalation attacks.

Audit Logging records all data access for forensic analysis and compliance. Logs should capture who accessed what data when and for what purpose. Tamper-evident log storage prevents attackers from covering their tracks.

Effective logging balances completeness with performance. Logging every byte access proves impractical. Logging only authentication events proves insufficient. Appropriate granularity logs meaningful operations like queries, model training runs, and inference batches.

Data Retention Policies limit how long data remains accessible. Retaining data indefinitely increases the impact of breaches and the regulatory compliance burden. Clear policies defining retention periods enable automatic deletion, minimizing exposure.

For machine learning, retention policies must balance model accuracy with privacy and security. Historical training data might enable model updates, but retaining it indefinitely creates privacy risks. Graduated retention policies might keep recent data accessible while archiving or deleting older data.

3.3 Secure Model Development

Training Infrastructure Security

Isolated Training Environments prevent training processes from affecting production systems. Training should occur in a dedicated infrastructure with network isolation from production. This prevents training-time compromises from spreading to operational systems.

Isolation extends to credentials and secrets. Training environments should use separate authentication credentials from those used in production. Compromising training credentials should not grant production access. Separate secret management for different environments provides additional isolation.

Secure Dependency Management addresses risks from third-party libraries. Training often requires numerous open-source libraries. Each dependency represents a potential attack vector. Security practices include:

- Dependency scanning for known vulnerabilities
- Version pinning to prevent automatic untrusted updates
- Software composition analysis tracking all transitive dependencies
- Internal mirroring of external repositories to prevent supply chain attacks
- Regular dependency updates to patch vulnerabilities

Automated tools should continuously scan dependencies, alerting teams to newly discovered vulnerabilities. Critical vulnerabilities must be remediated immediately before continuing development.

Hardware Security protects against physical attacks and side channels. Trusted execution environments such as Intel SGX or ARM TrustZone provide isolated execution for sensitive operations. Hardware security modules (HSMs) protect cryptographic keys.

For high-value models, training might occur on dedicated hardware never exposed to networks. Air-gapped training prevents remote attacks but increases operational complexity. Organizations must balance security benefits against usability costs.

Adversarial Training

Generating Adversarial Examples during training improves model robustness. The training process includes adversarial examples alongside normal training data, teaching models to correctly classify perturbed inputs.

Multiple adversarial example generation methods provide diverse training:

- Fast Gradient Sign Method for computational efficiency
- Projected Gradient Descent for stronger perturbations
- Carlini-Wagner attacks for minimal perturbations
- Diverse attack strategies to prevent overfitting to specific attacks

Adversarial training requires careful tuning. Too many adversarial examples can reduce accuracy on clean data. Too few provide insufficient robustness. Curriculum learning gradually increases the difficulty of adversarial examples during training.

Certified Defenses provide mathematical guarantees about model robustness. Techniques like randomized smoothing transform models to certify that predictions remain constant within specified input perturbation bounds. Certified defenses trade some accuracy for provable robustness guarantees.

While certified defenses provide strong theoretical guarantees, they face practical limitations. Certification typically applies to small perturbation bounds. Computational costs often exceed standard training. However, for safety-critical applications, provable robustness justifies these costs.

Robust Learning Algorithms

Outlier-Resistant Training tolerates limited data corruption. Traditional training minimizes average loss across all examples, allowing outliers to disproportionately influence learning. Robust training algorithms, such as Iteratively Reweighted Least Squares, downweight suspicious examples.

Trimmed loss functions discard the worst-performing examples before computing gradients. This prevents poisoned samples from dominating training. However, trimming risks discards legitimate, difficult examples. Careful tuning balances poisoning resistance with learning capacity.

Differential Privacy in Training adds noise during training to prevent memorization of individual examples. The noise makes models provably less likely to memorize training data, providing privacy guarantees while maintaining utility.

Differential privacy requires careful parameter selection. Privacy budgets control the amount of noise added, trading privacy for accuracy. Tighter privacy budgets provide stronger guarantees but reduce model performance. Applications must balance privacy requirements against accuracy needs.

Federated Learning enables training on distributed data without centralization. Each participant trains on local data and shares only model updates, not raw data. Aggregating updates creates global models while preserving local data privacy.

Federated learning faces security challenges posed by malicious participants who submit corrupted updates. Secure aggregation protocols prevent the aggregator from seeing individual updates. Byzantine-robust aggregation algorithms tolerate malicious participants. However, perfect Byzantine tolerance remains challenging at scale.

3.4 Security Testing and Validation

Adversarial Robustness Testing

Automated Attack Generation systematically tests model robustness. Tools like CleverHans and Foolbox generate adversarial examples using multiple attack algorithms. Testing should cover a range of attack strengths and strategies.

Robustness testing extends beyond adversarial examples to include:

- Distribution shift testing with out-of-distribution inputs
- Worst-case input testing exploring edge cases
- Stress testing with unusual but valid inputs
- Compositional testing combining multiple perturbation types

Comprehensive testing reveals brittleness that targeted adversarial training might miss.

Red Team Exercises involve security experts attacking systems using any available techniques. Red teams think like adversaries, combining automated tools with creative manual attacks. Their goal is to break systems to reveal vulnerabilities before real attackers do.

Effective red teaming requires an adversarial mindset and deep technical knowledge. Red teams should have access to system internals to thoroughly test defenses. However, black-box testing also provides valuable insights into vulnerabilities that can be exploited through public interfaces.

Backdoor Detection

Neural Cleanse techniques reverse-engineer potential backdoor triggers. These methods search for small perturbations that consistently misclassify specific target classes. Finding such triggers suggests a backdoor presence.

Backdoor detection faces challenges in distinguishing malicious triggers from natural model sensitivities. Comprehensive testing requires checking all possible source-target class pairs. For models with many classes, this becomes computationally expensive.

Activation Clustering analyzes hidden layer activations for backdoored inputs. Backdoor examples might cluster separately from clean examples in activation space. Clustering algorithms identify suspicious groupings warranting investigation.

This approach requires collecting representative clean data for comparison. Without good baselines, distinguishing backdoors from natural variation proves difficult. Multiple complementary techniques improve detection reliability.

Privacy Auditing

Membership Inference Testing evaluates whether attackers can determine if specific examples appeared in training data. Running membership inference attacks against your own models quantifies privacy leakage.

Testing should use multiple attack variants with varying assumptions about the attacker's knowledge. Strong privacy protection should resist all tested attacks. Failure indicates privacy vulnerabilities requiring mitigation through differential privacy or other techniques.

Model Inversion Testing attempts to reconstruct training data from model outputs. Successfully extracting recognizable training examples indicates serious privacy vulnerabilities. Testing should use state-of-the-art inversion techniques to identify worst-case risks.

For language models, testing should attempt to extract memorized text, including personally identifiable information. Automated scanning can identify common patterns, such as phone numbers and email addresses, in model outputs.

3.5 Secure Deployment

Deployment Architecture

Containerization and Orchestration isolate inference services from the underlying infrastructure. Containers like Docker package models with dependencies, ensuring consistent deployment. Kubernetes orchestrates containers, managing scaling and failure recovery.

Security hardening for containers includes:

- Minimal base images reducing attack surface
- Non-root user processes preventing privilege escalation
- Read-only filesystems preventing runtime modification
- Network policies restricting inter-service communication
- Resource limits preventing denial of service

Container security requires ongoing maintenance. Base images need regular updates to patch vulnerabilities. Security scanning should run continuously against deployed containers.

API Security protects inference endpoints from attacks. Security mechanisms include:

- Strong authentication requiring credentials for all requests
- Authorization verifying permissions for each operation
- Input validation rejecting malformed or adversarial inputs
- Rate limiting, preventing extraction, and denial of service
- Output filtering prevents information leakage
- Request logging enabling forensic analysis

APIs should return minimal information necessary for functionality. Confidence scores across all classes enable extraction attacks more easily than single-class predictions. Careful API design balances utility with security.

Model Versioning and Rollback

Version Control for Models tracks changes over time. Every deployed model should have a unique version identifier. Version control enables:

- Tracking which model version serves production traffic
- Rolling back to previous versions when issues arise

- Auditing model changes for compliance
- Testing specific versions in staging before production

Model registries provide centralized version management. They store model artifacts with metadata, including training data version, hyperparameters, and performance metrics. Immutable storage prevents unauthorized modification.

Gradual Rollout deploys new models incrementally. Rather than immediately switching all traffic to new models, a gradual rollout gradually increases the percentage of traffic to new versions. This enables detecting issues before full deployment.

Canary deployments initially send small traffic percentages to new models. Monitoring compares the new model behavior against the baseline. If metrics remain acceptable, traffic gradually increases. Anomalies trigger automatic rollback, containing damage.

Monitoring and Alerting

Performance Monitoring tracks model accuracy and latency. Degradation might indicate attacks or a distribution shift. Separate monitoring for different user segments detects targeted attacks affecting specific populations.

Metrics to monitor include:

- Prediction accuracy on test sets
- Inference latency percentiles
- Error rates and types
- Resource utilization
- API response codes

Dashboards visualize metrics in real-time. Automated alerts notify teams of anomalies. Playbooks define response procedures for common alert types.

Behavioral Monitoring detects unusual model behavior. Sudden changes in prediction distributions might indicate compromise. Unusual query patterns might signal extraction attacks. Spikes in specific error types warrant investigation.

Machine learning can monitor machine learning. Anomaly detection systems trained on normal model behavior flag deviations. However, these meta-models introduce additional complexity and their own security considerations.

Security Information and Event Management (SIEM) aggregates security logs from across the system. SIEM platforms correlate events from multiple sources, detecting sophisticated attacks that span multiple systems.

For AI systems, SIEM ingests:

- Authentication and authorization logs
- API request logs with inputs and outputs
- Model training logs
- System resource utilization
- Network traffic logs

Correlation rules identify attack patterns, such as extraction attempts or privilege escalation. Machine learning enhances SIEM by learning normal patterns and flagging anomalies.

3.6 Continuous Security Improvement

Incident Response

Preparation establishes procedures before incidents occur. Incident response plans define:

- Roles and responsibilities during incidents
- Communication channels and escalation procedures

- Forensic data collection requirements
- Containment and remediation procedures
- Post-incident review processes

Regular tabletop exercises test plans and keep teams prepared. Simulation scenarios covering different attack types ensure readiness.

Detection identifies security incidents quickly. Effective monitoring enables rapid detection, limiting damage. Detection mechanisms include:

- Automated alerts from monitoring systems
- User reports of unexpected behavior
- Security tool alerts
- Third-party vulnerability disclosures

On-call procedures ensure alerts receive prompt attention. Clear severity definitions guide response urgency.

Containment limits incident impact. Initial containment might involve:

- Rolling back to known-good model versions
- Disabling affected API endpoints
- Isolating compromised systems
- Revoking compromised credentials

Containment balances service availability against security. A complete service shutdown might prevent further damage, but it disrupts legitimate users. Targeted containment maintains service while addressing threats.

Recovery restores normal operations after addressing root causes. Recovery might require:

- Retraining models on validated clean data
- Patching infrastructure vulnerabilities
- Updating defensive mechanisms
- Restoring from backups

Validation before restoration ensures systems are genuinely secure. Rushing recovery risks reintroducing vulnerabilities.

Lessons Learned analyzes incidents to prevent recurrence. Post-incident reviews examine:

- How did the attack succeed?
- What detection mechanisms failed?
- What could improve the response?
- What systemic issues enabled the attack?

Insights from reviews inform security improvements. Organizations should share lessons learned with the broader community to improve industry-wide security.

Security Audits

Internal Audits regularly assess security posture. Audit scope includes:

- Access control policy compliance
- Data handling procedure adherence
- Model versioning and change management
- Security tool effectiveness
- Training and awareness programs

Internal audits identify gaps before external audits or real attacks. Regular cadence ensures continuous improvement rather than point-in-time compliance.

External Audits provide an independent assessment. Third-party auditors bring fresh perspectives and specialized expertise. External audits verify internal assessments and identify blind spots.

For regulated industries, external audits may be mandatory. Even without regulatory requirements, external validation provides assurance to stakeholders and customers.

Penetration Testing simulates real attacks. Professional penetration testers attempt to compromise systems using any available techniques. Unlike vulnerability scanning, which checks for known issues, penetration testing explores creative attack combinations.

Penetration testing should occur regularly and after significant changes. The test scope should cover the full system, including data pipelines, training infrastructure, and inference services. Reports should provide both executive summaries and detailed technical findings.

Security Training and Culture

Developer Training ensures teams understand security best practices. Training topics include:

- Common AI security vulnerabilities
- Secure coding practices
- Threat modeling techniques
- Security tool usage
- Incident response procedures

Training should be ongoing rather than one-time. New threats emerge continuously. Annual refresher training keeps skills current.

Security Champions embed security expertise throughout organizations. These developers receive advanced security training and serve as champion resources for their teams. Champions advocate for security during design and code review.

Security champions bridge the gap between security specialists and development teams. They translate security requirements into practical implementation guidance. Their distributed presence ensures security considerations reach all projects.

Culture of Security makes security everyone's responsibility and makes it known. Organizations should celebrate security improvements and learning from mistakes. Blame-free incident reviews focus on systemic improvements rather than individual failures.

Security metrics should track positive behaviors, such as vulnerability reports and security test coverage, rather than just negative indicators like incident counts. Positive reinforcement encourages security engagement.

Chapter Summary

This chapter provided comprehensive guidance for developing secure AI systems:

Security-by-Design: Fundamental security principles, including defense-in-depth, least privilege, and fail-safe defaults, guide secure system architecture. Threat modeling identifies risks and prioritizes defenses. Security patterns like isolation boundaries and zero-trust architecture provide proven solutions.

Data Security: Secure data management begins at collection with provenance tracking, source authentication, and integrity verification. Curation employs anomaly detection and label validation. Storage security includes encryption, access control, and audit logging.

Model Development: Secure training requires isolated environments, secure dependencies, and hardware security. Adversarial training and robust learning algorithms improve model resilience. Differential privacy and federated learning address privacy concerns.

Testing and Validation: Comprehensive testing includes adversarial robustness testing, backdoor detection, and privacy auditing. Red team exercises reveal vulnerabilities before real attackers exploit them.

Deployment Security: Secure deployment employs containerization, API security, and gradual rollout. Version control enables rollback when issues arise. Comprehensive monitoring detects attacks and performance degradation.

Continuous Improvement: Incident response procedures enable rapid reaction to breaches. Regular security audits identify gaps. Training and culture ensure security remains a priority across organizations.

Effective AI security requires sustained effort throughout the development lifecycle. No single technique provides complete protection. Layered defenses addressing multiple attack vectors create resilient systems.

Key Takeaways

1. Security must be designed into AI systems from inception rather than added post-development. Embedding security in early stages proves more effective and less costly than retrofitting.

2. Defense in depth provides resilience against diverse attacks. Multiple independent security layers ensure that no single failure compromises the entire system.

3. Data security forms the foundation of AI security. Compromised training data creates persistent vulnerabilities that survive into deployment regardless of other security measures.

4. Threat modeling helps prioritize security investments by identifying high-risk attack vectors specific to each system's architecture and deployment context.

5. Comprehensive testing must extend beyond functional correctness to include adversarial robustness, backdoor detection, and privacy auditing.

6. Deployment requires ongoing monitoring and incident response capabilities. Detection and rapid response limit damage when attacks succeed.

7. Security culture and continuous training ensure that security remains a priority as teams and technologies evolve.

Reflection Questions

1. Consider an organization developing a medical diagnosis AI system. How would you prioritize security investments across data collection, model training, and deployment phases?

2. What tensions exist between adversarial training that improves robustness and standard training that maximizes clean accuracy? How should organizations balance these competing objectives?

3. If you need to choose between encrypting training data at rest or implementing comprehensive audit logging, which provides better security? What factors inform this decision?

4. How does the security posture required for an AI system differ between deployment in a controlled enterprise environment versus deployment on consumer devices?

5. Compare the security implications of using pre-trained foundation models versus training models from scratch. What additional security considerations does transfer learning introduce?

6. If monitoring systems detect anomalous model behavior but cannot definitively confirm an attack, what response is appropriate? How do you balance security caution against service availability?

4

Ethics, Fairness, and Regulatory Compliance

Learning Objectives

By the end of this chapter, you will:

- Understand the ethical dimensions of AI security and their relationship to technical implementation
- Identify sources of bias in AI systems and implement mitigation strategies
- Navigate the evolving regulatory landscape across different jurisdictions
- Design accountability frameworks that enable auditing and redress
- Apply fairness metrics to evaluate AI system outcomes across demographic groups
- Develop compliance strategies that balance innovation with regulatory requirements
- Implement transparency mechanisms that build stakeholder trust

Introduction: Where Security Meets Society

AI security extends beyond protecting systems from technical attacks. Secure AI systems must also operate ethically, treat people fairly, and comply with evolving regulations. A technically robust system that discriminates against protected groups fails at security in the broadest sense. A system that violates privacy regulations creates legal and reputational risks regardless of its adversarial robustness.

This chapter explores the intersection of security, ethics, and regulation. We examine how ethical principles inform security design, how fairness requirements shape implementation decisions, and how regulatory compliance influences architectural choices. The goal is not to present ethics and regulation as constraints on security but as integral components of comprehensive AI security strategies.

The ethical and regulatory landscape continues evolving rapidly. Frameworks that seemed theoretical five years ago now carry legal force. Organizations must proactively address these concerns rather than reacting to enforcement actions. This chapter provides guidance for building systems that meet both technical security requirements and societal expectations.

4.1 Ethical Foundations of AI Security

The Expanded Security Paradigm

Traditional cybersecurity focuses on confidentiality, integrity, and availability. AI security must expand this paradigm to include fairness, accountability, and transparency. This expansion recognizes that AI systems make consequential decisions affecting people's lives. Security that protects systems while harming people represents a hollow victory.

Fairness as Security treats discriminatory outcomes as security failures. An AI hiring system biased against women constitutes a security vulnerability just as serious as one susceptible to adversarial examples.

Both compromise system integrity and create harm. Security frameworks must incorporate fairness metrics alongside traditional measures.

Accountability as Defense requires systems that enable auditing and provide recourse when harm occurs. Black box models that resist explanation create accountability failures. Users affected by AI decisions deserve explanations and mechanisms for appeal. Accountability transforms from an abstract principle to a concrete technical requirement.

Transparency as Trust recognizes that security depends partly on user trust. Systems that operate in an opaque manner generate suspicion even when functioning correctly. Transparent disclosure of capabilities, limitations, and decision-making processes builds trust, enabling effective security measures.

Ethical Principles for AI Security

Several ethical principles guide secure AI development:

Beneficence requires systems to benefit users and society. AI security measures should enhance rather than undermine human welfare. Security measures that render systems unusable violate this principle. Effective security enables beneficial AI applications by preventing misuse and building trust.

Non-Maleficence obligates systems to avoid causing harm. This principle extends beyond obvious harms, such as privacy violations, to include subtle harms, including the reinforcement of stereotypes. Security designs must assess potential harms across diverse populations, not just average users.

Autonomy respects human agency and decision-making capacity. AI systems should augment human judgment rather than replace it for consequential decisions. Security measures should preserve human control while preventing malicious automation.

Justice demands fair distribution of AI benefits and burdens. Security measures should not disproportionately burden disadvantaged groups. For example, aggressive facial recognition security might create greater surveillance of minority communities. Justice requires evaluating security impacts across populations.

Explicability requires providing understandable explanations for AI decisions. Users deserve to understand how systems reach conclusions affecting them. Security implementations must preserve explainability rather than treating opacity as an acceptable trade-off for performance.

Ethical Risk Assessment

Organizations should assess ethical risks alongside technical security risks:

Stakeholder Identification catalogs all parties affected by AI systems. Stakeholders extend beyond direct users to include people subject to AI decisions without direct interaction, communities affected by aggregate system impacts, workers displaced by AI automation, future generations inheriting AI-shaped systems, and marginalized groups potentially harmed by bias.

A comprehensive stakeholder analysis ensures ethical assessment considers all affected parties, not just obvious users.

Value Elicitation determines what matters to different stakeholders. Different groups prioritize different values. Privacy-conscious users might value data minimization. Efficiency-focused organizations might prioritize performance. Fairness advocates might emphasize equitable outcomes.

Elicitation techniques include surveys, focus groups, and participatory design. Engaging diverse stakeholders reveals value tensions that require deliberate trade-offs rather than implicit prioritization of developer preferences.

Impact Analysis examines how systems affect different stakeholders. Analysis should consider direct effects on individuals interacting with systems, indirect effects on people influenced by system outputs, aggregate effects on communities and institutions, long-term effects as systems shape future environments, and differential effects across demographic groups.

Impact analysis reveals ethical risks that inform design decisions. High-impact systems warrant more extensive ethical scrutiny and stakeholder involvement.

Mitigation Strategy Development addresses identified ethical risks. Strategies might include technical interventions such as debiasing algorithms, process interventions such as human review for high-stakes decisions, policy interventions such as usage restrictions, transparency interventions such as explainability requirements, and governance interventions such as oversight committees.

No single strategy addresses all ethical risks. Layered approaches combining multiple interventions prove most effective.

4.2 Fairness in AI Systems

Understanding Bias

Bias in AI systems originates from multiple sources requiring different mitigation approaches:

Historical Bias exists in training data reflecting past discrimination. A hiring model trained on historical decisions perpetuates past biases. Medical models trained on predominantly male patients perform worse for female patients. Historical bias cannot be eliminated through technical means alone without addressing underlying data issues.

Representation Bias occurs when training data inadequately represents certain groups. Facial recognition systems trained predominantly on light-skinned faces perform worse on dark-skinned faces. Underrepresentation creates performance disparities that constitute unfairness.

Measurement Bias arises from how concepts get operationalized in data. Using arrest records as crime proxies introduces bias because arrest rates reflect policing patterns, not just crime rates. Biased measurements propagate through entire systems regardless of algorithmic fairness.

Aggregation Bias emerges from treating diverse populations as homogeneous. One-size-fits-all models may perform well on average while performing poorly for minority groups. Aggregation bias suggests models should account for population diversity.

Evaluation Bias results from testing on unrepresentative data. Models evaluated only on majority-group data may appear accurate while failing on minority groups. Comprehensive evaluation requires diverse test sets.

Deployment Bias occurs when systems are used in contexts different from training. A model developed in one demographic context may fail when deployed in different contexts. Deployment bias requires careful validation before applying models to new populations.

Fairness Metrics

Multiple mathematical definitions of fairness exist, often with tensions between them:

Demographic Parity requires equal positive outcome rates across groups. A loan approval system satisfies demographic parity if approval rates match across racial groups. This definition treats equal outcomes as fairness regardless of differences in applicant qualifications.

Equalized Odds requires equal true-positive and false-positive rates across groups. A diagnostic system satisfies equalized odds if it correctly identifies disease at equal rates and incorrectly diagnoses healthy people at equal rates across demographic groups. This definition balances sensitivity and specificity across populations.

Equal Opportunity requires equal true positive rates across groups. This relaxed version of equalized odds focuses on ensuring qualified individuals receive positive outcomes at equal rates across groups.

Predictive Parity requires equal positive predictive value across groups. Among those receiving positive predictions, the fraction truly positive should be equal across groups. This ensures predictions have equal meaning across populations.

Calibration requires predicted probabilities to match actual frequencies across groups. If a model assigns a 70% loan default probability to applicants, approximately 70% of them should default, regardless of demographic group. Calibration ensures probability estimates mean the same across populations.

Individual Fairness requires treating similar individuals similarly. People with similar qualifications should receive similar outcomes regardless of group membership. This definition focuses on individual treatment rather than group statistics.

Tensions exist between these definitions. A system satisfying demographic parity may violate equalized odds. A system satisfying calibration may violate predictive parity. Organizations must choose fairness metrics aligned with their values and application context.

Bias Mitigation Strategies

Pre-Processing Techniques address bias before training:

Data Rebalancing adjusts training set composition to ensure adequate representation. Oversampling minority groups or undersampling majority groups creates more balanced datasets. However, rebalancing must avoid introducing artificial patterns.

Data Augmentation generates synthetic examples to increase minority representation. Careful augmentation preserves realistic data characteristics while increasing diversity. Poor augmentation creates unrealistic examples that degrade model quality.

Bias-Aware Sampling weights training examples to counteract bias. Examples from underrepresented groups receive higher weights, increasing their influence on training. This approach requires less synthetic data than augmentation.

In-Processing Techniques modify training to promote fairness:

Adversarial Debiasing trains models to make accurate predictions while preventing auxiliary networks from predicting protected attributes. The model learns representations that preserve task-relevant information while removing demographic information.

Prejudice Remover adds regularization terms penalizing dependence on protected attributes. The regularization balances accuracy with fairness, with hyperparameters controlling the trade-off.

Fair Representation Learning learns intermediate representations that enable accurate predictions while satisfying fairness constraints. These representations can be used with any downstream classifier.

Post-Processing Techniques adjust outputs to achieve fairness:

Threshold Optimization selects distinct classification thresholds for each group to satisfy fairness constraints. This approach can achieve various fairness definitions without retraining models.

Calibration adjusts predicted probabilities to ensure equal calibration across groups. This technique specifically addresses calibration fairness but may affect other fairness metrics.

Fair Ranking reorders system outputs to promote fairness. Search results or recommendation lists can be reranked to ensure fair representation while maintaining relevance.

Fairness-Security Trade-offs

Fairness and security interact in complex ways:

Adversarial Fairness recognizes that adversaries might exploit fairness constraints. If a system ensures demographic parity, adversaries might game protected attribute distributions to manipulate outcomes. Fairness-aware security must consider such attacks.

Fairness Auditing Risks create potential vulnerabilities. Detailed fairness audits reveal model behavior that might enable attacks. Organizations must balance transparency with security when publishing audit results.

Privacy-Fairness Tensions arise because fairness assessment requires demographic information, while privacy protection limits data collection. Differential privacy particularly complicates fairness auditing. Organizations must navigate these tensions carefully.

Robustness-Fairness Trade-offs occur because adversarial training often reduces fairness. Models trained for robustness may exhibit greater bias. Achieving both robustness and fairness requires careful algorithm design.

4.3 The Regulatory Landscape

Global Regulatory Frameworks

European Union AI Act represents a comprehensive AI regulation establishing a risk-based framework:

Prohibited Applications ban certain AI uses deemed unacceptable risks, including government social scoring systems, real-time biometric identification in public spaces (with limited exceptions), subliminal manipulation that causes harm, and exploitation of vulnerable groups.

High-Risk Applications require extensive compliance for systems affecting critical infrastructure, education and employment, law enforcement, justice and democratic processes, and biometric identification.

High-risk systems must demonstrate conformity through documentation, risk management, data governance, transparency, human oversight, and cybersecurity measures.

Limited Risk Applications face transparency requirements. Users must know they interact with AI systems. Deepfakes must be labeled. Emotion recognition and biometric categorization require user disclosure.

Minimal Risk Applications, such as spam filters, face no specific requirements beyond existing regulations.

The General Data Protection Regulation (GDPR) establishes data protection requirements affecting AI:

Lawful Basis requirements mean AI systems must identify legal justification for processing personal data. Consent, contract performance, legal obligation, vital interests, public task, or legitimate interests provide potential bases.

Purpose Limitation restricts data use beyond the originally specified purposes. Training models on personal data requires clear purpose statements. Repurposing data for new models may require an additional legal basis.

Data Minimization requires collecting only necessary data for specified purposes. AI systems should not hoard data speculatively. This principle conflicts with machine learning preferences for abundant data.

Right to Explanation may require explaining automated decision-making. While GDPR does not explicitly guarantee the right to explanation, it requires that meaningful information be provided about automated decision-making. This affects opaque AI systems.

Data Portability enables individuals to receive and transfer their data. AI systems must support data export in structured formats, potentially including model predictions about individuals.

The Right to Erasure allows individuals to request the deletion of their data. For AI systems, this creates challenges when training data becomes embedded in model parameters. The extent to which erasure requires retraining remains legally unclear.

United States Regulatory Approach

The US lacks comprehensive federal AI regulation but has sector-specific requirements:

Algorithmic Accountability legislation under consideration would require impact assessments for high-risk systems. Proposed requirements include documentation, testing, mitigation plans, and ongoing monitoring.

Fair Lending Laws, such as the Equal Credit Opportunity Act, prohibit discrimination in lending. AI credit scoring models must comply with fair lending requirements regardless of algorithm opacity.

Fair Housing Laws prohibit discrimination in housing decisions. AI systems for tenant screening or property valuation must avoid disparate impact on protected groups.

Employment Discrimination Laws under Title VII restrict employment decisions. AI hiring and promotion systems must not discriminate based on protected characteristics.

FTC Authority over unfair and deceptive practices extends to AI systems. False performance claims or inadequate security constitute violations of the FTC Act.

State-Level Regulations increasingly address AI. California's Delete Act extends data deletion rights. New York City requires bias audits for hiring algorithms under NYC Local Law 144 (2021). State regulations create compliance complexity for multi-state operations.

Sector-Specific Regulations

Healthcare faces extensive regulation affecting AI:

HIPAA requires protecting the confidentiality, integrity, and availability of health information. AI systems processing health data must implement appropriate safeguards and enable patient access rights.

FDA Oversight of medical devices extends to AI/ML-enabled devices. Software-as-a-Medical-Device regulations require demonstrating safety and effectiveness. Continuously learning models face additional oversight challenges.

Clinical Validation requirements mean medical AI must demonstrate clinical utility through rigorous testing. Performance on benchmark datasets proves insufficient. Real-world validation in clinical settings becomes necessary.

Financial Services regulations affect AI extensively:

Regulatory Model Risk Management guidance requires comprehensive validation, ongoing monitoring, and documentation. AI models face scrutiny comparable to traditional statistical models.

Fair Lending Compliance requires demonstrating that credit models do not discriminate. Model explainability helps demonstrate compliance, but may not suffice if disparate impact exists.

Anti-Money Laundering systems using AI must balance detection effectiveness with minimizing false positives affecting legitimate customers.

4.4 Building Accountable AI Systems

Explainability and Interpretability

Model-Agnostic Explanation Methods work with any model:

LIME (Local Interpretable Model-agnostic Explanations) approximates complex models locally with interpretable models. For any prediction, LIME identifies which features most influenced the decision by testing perturbations.

SHAP (Shapley Additive exPlanations) assigns feature importance values using game-theoretic methods. SHAP values indicate how much each feature contributed to moving the prediction from baseline to final value.

Counterfactual Explanations identify minimal input changes that would alter predictions. Showing that changing specific features affects outcomes helps users understand decision logic.

Model-Specific Explanation Methods leverage architecture knowledge:

Attention Visualization for transformers shows which inputs receive attention when generating outputs. Attention patterns reveal which context the model considers relevant.

Gradient-Based Saliency identifies input regions most influential on predictions. Gradient magnitude indicates sensitivity to local changes, revealing important input features.

Layer-wise Relevance Propagation backpropagates prediction relevance through network layers, attributing importance to input features through a computational graph.

Documentation and Transparency

Model Cards provide standardized documentation, including intended use cases and limitations; training data characteristics and known biases; performance metrics across demographic groups; ethical considerations and known risks; and testing procedures and results.

Model cards enable informed decisions about whether models are suited to specific applications. They facilitate accountability by documenting known limitations.

Datasheets for Datasets document training data characteristics: motivation for dataset creation, composition and collection procedures, preprocessing and labeling procedures, recommended uses and limitations, and distribution and maintenance plans.

Datasheets help practitioners understand dataset suitability and limitations, preventing inappropriate use.

System Cards describe complete AI systems, including system purpose and use cases, components and data flows, stakeholders and their roles, known limitations and failure modes, testing and validation procedures, and monitoring and update procedures.

System cards provide comprehensive documentation supporting auditing and accountability.

Governance Structures

Ethics Review Boards evaluate AI systems before deployment:

Boards should include diverse membership spanning technical experts, domain specialists, ethicists, legal counsel, and community representatives. This diversity ensures a comprehensive perspective on ethical implications.

Review processes should examine use cases, potential harms, fairness considerations, privacy implications, and mitigation strategies. High-risk systems require more extensive review than low-risk applications.

Algorithmic Impact Assessments systematically evaluate AI effects:

Assessments document system purpose and functionality, affected populations, potential benefits and harms, fairness considerations, privacy implications, security measures, mitigation strategies, and monitoring plans.

Regular reassessment ensures continued appropriateness as systems and contexts evolve.

Audit Mechanisms enable verification of AI system properties:

Internal Audits conducted by organizations provide an ongoing assessment. Auditors examine documentation, test systems, review decision records, and interview stakeholders.

External Audits by independent parties provide an objective evaluation. Third-party auditors bring specialized expertise and credibility through independence.

Continuous Auditing through automated monitoring enables real-time assessment. Systems can automatically track fairness metrics, performance indicators, and anomaly detection signals.

4.5 Privacy Regulation and AI

Privacy-Preserving AI Techniques

Differential Privacy provides mathematical privacy guarantees:

Adding calibrated noise to training data or model outputs ensures individual data points have a limited influence on results. Privacy budgets quantify privacy loss, enabling principled trade-offs between privacy and utility.

Implementations include input perturbation, adding noise before training, gradient perturbation, adding noise during training, and output perturbation, adding noise to predictions.

Federated Learning enables distributed training:

Data remains on local devices or servers. Only model updates transfer to central aggregators. This prevents exposure of raw data while enabling collaborative learning.

Security enhancements include secure aggregation, preventing coordinators from seeing individual updates, differential privacy for updates that provides formal guarantees, and Byzantine-robust aggregation that tolerates malicious participants.

Homomorphic Encryption enables computation on encrypted data:

Systems can perform inference on encrypted inputs, producing encrypted outputs that only users can decrypt. This prevents service providers from accessing user data.

Practical limitations include computational overhead and restricted operation sets. Fully homomorphic encryption remains expensive, but partially homomorphic schemes are well-suited to specific applications.

Secure Multi-Party Computation enables joint computation:

Multiple parties can collaboratively train models without revealing individual datasets. Cryptographic protocols ensure no party learns others' private data.

Applications include cross-institution medical research, multi-bank fraud detection, and collaborative business intelligence.

Privacy Compliance Strategies

Privacy by Design integrates privacy throughout development:

Data Minimization collects only necessary information. Systems should justify each data element's necessity. Default configurations should minimize data collection.

Purpose Specification clearly defines processing purposes. Using data beyond stated purposes requires additional consent or a legal basis.

Transparency informs users about data practices. Privacy policies should explain what data is collected, why, how it's used, and how long it's retained.

User Control provides meaningful choices. Users should control data sharing, processing preferences, and deletion. Controls should be accessible and understandable.

Security Safeguards protect personal data. Encryption, access controls, and monitoring prevent unauthorized access.

Accountability assigns responsibility for privacy. Organizations must demonstrate compliance through documentation and governance.

4.6 Case Studies in Ethics and Compliance

Note: The following case studies are based on well-documented real-world incidents in AI systems. They are presented for educational purposes to illustrate ethical and compliance challenges. Specific organizational names have been generalized where appropriate to focus on lessons learned rather than attribution.

Case Study 1: Biased Hiring Algorithm

A major technology company deployed AI for resume screening. Analysis revealed the system penalized resumes mentioning women's colleges or female-associated extracurriculars. The bias emerged from training on historical hiring data reflecting past discrimination.

Root Cause: Historical hiring patterns overrepresented male candidates. The model learned to associate male indicators with hiring success.

Immediate Response: The company suspended the system and commissioned an external audit. Investigation revealed multiple proxies for gender beyond obvious indicators.

Remediation: The organization rebuilt the system with rebalanced training data, ensuring gender diversity; fairness constraints requiring equal consideration across groups; adversarial debiasing to remove gender information from representations; regular fairness audits comparing outcomes across demographics; and human review for all hiring decisions.

Lessons Learned: Removing explicit protected attributes proves insufficient. Models find proxies through correlated features. Comprehensive fairness requires proactive measures throughout development.

Case Study 2: Facial Recognition Accuracy Disparities

Research revealed that commercial facial recognition systems exhibited significant accuracy disparities across demographic groups. Systems performed substantially worse on dark-skinned and female faces compared to light-skinned male faces.

Root Cause: Training datasets inadequately represented diverse demographics. Many systems are trained predominantly on light-skinned male faces.

Industry Impact: Findings triggered industry-wide reevaluation of facial recognition fairness. Several vendors withdrew systems pending improvement.

Remediation Strategies: Dataset diversification, ensuring demographic representation, disaggregated evaluation reporting performance by demographic group, minimum performance requirements across all groups, and use case restrictions limiting deployment where disparities create harm.

Regulatory Response: Several jurisdictions banned or restricted facial recognition use based on fairness concerns. Others mandated accuracy standards across demographics.

Ongoing Challenges: Representation alone proves insufficient. System design, feature engineering, and evaluation procedures all affect fairness.

Case Study 3: Algorithmic Risk Assessment in Criminal Justice

Law enforcement and judicial systems deployed AI to assess recidivism risk for bail and sentencing decisions. Analysis revealed systems exhibited racial disparities, potentially reinforcing discriminatory patterns.

Root Cause: Training data reflected historical criminal justice patterns rather than true recidivism distributions. Models potentially amplified existing biases.

Ethical Concerns: Feedback loops where predictions influence decisions that generate data confirming predictions, constitutional questions about algorithmic due process, community trust erosion from perceived discrimination, and accountability concerns about algorithmic decisions without human review.

Reform Efforts: Algorithmic audits evaluating fairness and accuracy, judicial oversight reviewing system use, transparency requirements documenting methodology, and use restrictions limiting deployment contexts.

Ongoing Debate: Fundamental questions remain about whether risk assessment algorithms can achieve fairness given potentially biased historical data. Some jurisdictions have substantially limited or discontinued use of these systems.

Case Study 4: Healthcare AI and Privacy

A healthcare provider's research division used patient data to train diagnostic AI without specific research consent. When researchers published results including model details, privacy advocates expressed concern about potential re-identification risks.

Privacy Concerns: Using medical data beyond treatment purposes without adequate authorization, insufficient de-identification before research use, publication potentially enabling re-identification attacks, and model memorization of sensitive patient information.

Regulatory Response: Regulators' investigation raised concerns about compliance with HIPAA requirements for research authorization and data protection.

Remediation: Enhanced consent procedures for research use, differential privacy implementation protecting individual patients, federated learning approaches keeping data within institutions, and privacy impact assessments for all AI projects.

Industry Impact: The incident catalyzed the development of privacy standards for healthcare AI. Professional societies issued guidelines for privacy-preserving medical AI research.

Case Study 5: Automated Content Moderation

Social media platforms deployed AI for content moderation at scale. Analysis revealed systems disproportionately flagged content from certain linguistic and cultural communities, potentially affecting legitimate expression.

Challenges: Training data reflecting majority cultural norms; difficulty distinguishing context-dependent meaning; balancing preventing harm and protecting expression; and scale requirements that prevent purely human moderation.

Fairness Issues: Higher false positive rates for non-dominant languages and dialects, cultural context misunderstanding leading to inappropriate flags, and satire and context-dependent meaning causing errors.

Ongoing Solutions: Culturally diverse training data and evaluation, human review with cultural competence, appeals processes for moderation decisions, and transparency reports on moderation accuracy by the community.

Remaining Tensions: Content moderation inherently involves value judgments that resist purely technical solutions. Balancing expression protection, user safety, and fairness remains challenging.

4.7 Compliance Implementation Strategies

Regulatory Intelligence

Monitoring Regulatory Developments ensures awareness of new requirements:

Organizations should track proposed legislation at the federal, state, and local levels, regulatory guidance from enforcement agencies, international regulatory developments affecting operations, and industry standards and best practices.

Dedicated regulatory monitoring or subscription services provide systematic tracking. Legal counsel should interpret implications for specific contexts.

Impact Assessment evaluates how regulations affect AI systems:

New regulations may require updates to documentation, additional testing, architectural changes, process modifications, and new governance structures.

Early impact assessment enables proactive compliance rather than reactive responses when regulations take effect.

Compliance Management Systems

Policy Development translates regulations into organizational requirements:

Policies should specify applicable regulations and standards, responsible parties for compliance, required procedures and controls, documentation requirements, and review and update cycles.

Policies provide clear guidance for development teams, reducing compliance burden through systematization.

Control Implementation operationalizes compliance requirements:

Controls include technical controls such as audit logging and access restrictions, process controls such as review gates and approvals, and documentation controls such as required assessments and reports.

Automated controls reduce compliance burden while improving consistency.

Compliance Testing verifies control effectiveness:

Regular testing ensures controls operate as intended. Testing approaches include manual testing of sample transactions, automated testing of technical controls, process audits validating procedure adherence, and external audits providing independent validation.

Continuous Monitoring detects compliance drift:

Automated monitoring tracks key compliance indicators. Alerts notify teams when metrics exceed thresholds or controls fail. Dashboards provide visibility into compliance posture.

Documentation and Reporting

Comprehensive Documentation supports compliance demonstration:

Required documentation includes system design and architecture documents, data flow diagrams and provenance records, risk assessments and mitigation plans, testing results and validation reports, monitoring data and incident records, and review meeting minutes and decisions.

Documentation proves compliance with regulators and enables internal accountability.

Regulatory Reporting fulfills disclosure requirements:

Some regulations require regular reporting. Reports might include algorithmic impact assessments, fairness metrics across demographics, incident disclosures, and compliance certifications.

Clear reporting processes ensure timely, accurate submissions.

Chapter Summary

This chapter explored the ethical, fairness, and regulatory dimensions of AI security:

Ethical Foundations: AI security must expand beyond traditional confidentiality, integrity, and availability to include fairness, accountability, and transparency. Ethical principles, including beneficence, non-maleficence, autonomy, justice, and explicability, guide secure AI development. Ethical risk assessment identifies potential harms across diverse stakeholders.

Fairness: Bias originates from multiple sources, including historical data, underrepresentation, biased measurement, and problematic aggregation. Multiple fairness metrics exist with tensions between them. Mitigation strategies span pre-processing data, modifying training, and post-processing outputs. Fairness and security interact in complex ways requiring careful design.

Regulatory Landscape: The EU AI Act, GDPR, and sector-specific regulations create compliance requirements. The US lacks comprehensive federal regulation but has sector-specific rules and increasing state-level requirements. Organizations must navigate multiple overlapping regulatory frameworks.

Accountability: Explainability techniques such as LIME, SHAP, and counterfactual explanations help make AI decisions more understandable. Documentation through model cards, datasheets, and system cards supports accountability. Governance structures, including ethics review boards and impact assessments, provide oversight.

Privacy: Techniques including differential privacy, federated learning, homomorphic encryption, and secure multi-party computation enable privacy-preserving AI. Privacy by design integrates protection throughout the development process.

Case Studies: Real-world examples, including biased hiring algorithms, facial recognition disparities, algorithmic risk assessment issues, healthcare privacy concerns, and content moderation challenges, illustrate ethical and compliance challenges. These cases provide lessons for avoiding similar problems.

Compliance Implementation: Systematic approaches to regulatory intelligence, compliance management, and documentation enable efficient compliance with requirements. Proactive compliance proves more effective than reactive responses to enforcement.

Key Takeaways

1. AI security must address ethical dimensions, including fairness and accountability, not just technical robustness. Discrimination and opacity constitute security failures.

2. Multiple fairness definitions exist with inherent tensions. Organizations must choose metrics aligned with their values and application context rather than assuming universal fairness.

3. Bias has multiple sources requiring different mitigation approaches. Technical debiasing alone proves insufficient without addressing data quality and measurement issues.

4. The regulatory landscape continues evolving rapidly. Organizations must proactively monitor developments and assess implications, rather than react to enforcement.

5. Transparency and explainability enable accountability but must balance security and intellectual property considerations. Appropriate transparency depends on stakeholder needs and risk levels.

6. Privacy-preserving techniques enable beneficial AI applications while protecting sensitive information. Privacy and utility need not completely conflict with proper technical implementation.

7. Real-world case studies demonstrate that ethical failures have serious consequences, including regulatory penalties, reputational damage, and user harm. Proactive ethical consideration proves far less costly than reactive remediation.

Reflection Questions

1. Consider a loan approval AI system. What fairness metric is most appropriate for this application? How would you justify your choice to different stakeholders?

2. How should organizations balance transparency requirements that enable accountability with security concerns that favor opacity? What factors inform this trade-off?

3. If achieving fairness requires collecting protected attribute information while privacy protection limits such collection, how do you resolve this tension?

4. Compare compliance costs between proactive ethical design from project inception versus reactive remediation after deployment. What factors influence this cost comparison?

5. When regulations conflict across jurisdictions (e.g., EU requirements versus US practices), what strategies enable complying with multiple frameworks simultaneously?

6. If explainability techniques reduce model accuracy, how do you determine acceptable trade-offs? What factors should inform decisions about sacrificing performance for interpretability?

5

Building Robust Defenses for AI Systems

Learning Objectives

By the end of this chapter, you will:

- Implement adversarial training techniques that improve model robustness
- Deploy input validation and sanitization mechanisms for inference systems
- Apply defensive distillation and other model hardening techniques
- Design ensemble architectures that provide defense through diversity
- Implement runtime monitoring systems that detect attacks in production
- Deploy certified defenses providing provable robustness guarantees
- Establish incident response procedures for AI security breaches
- Evaluate defense effectiveness through comprehensive testing

Introduction: From Reactive to Proactive Defense

Previous chapters explored the threat landscape and secure development practices. This chapter focuses specifically on defensive techniques that harden AI systems against attacks. We examine both preventive measures that make attacks more difficult and detective measures that identify attacks in progress.

AI defense requires layered approaches. No single technique provides complete protection against all attack vectors. An effective defense combines multiple complementary techniques that address different phases of attack and leverage distinct defensive principles. Some defenses prevent attacks from succeeding. Others detect attacks, enabling rapid response. Still others limit damage when attacks breach initial defenses.

The defensive techniques presented here span the AI lifecycle from training through deployment and operation. Some defenses require modifying training procedures. Others operate during inference. Some work at the model level while others function at the system level. Comprehensive protection requires selecting appropriate defenses for specific threat models and deployment contexts.

We emphasize practical implementation throughout this chapter. Each defensive technique includes a discussion of effectiveness, computational costs, implementation considerations, and some limitations. Understanding these trade-offs enables informed decisions about which defenses to deploy for particular applications.

5.1 Adversarial Training

Fundamental Concepts

Adversarial training improves model robustness by incorporating adversarial examples into the training process. The intuition is straightforward: if models train on perturbed inputs, they learn to classify them correctly. This approach directly addresses the brittleness that enables adversarial attacks.

The training process alternates between two phases. First, generate adversarial examples for the current training data using the current model. Second, train on both clean and adversarial examples. This process repeats throughout training, continuously updating adversarial examples as the model improves.

Adversarial training fundamentally changes the optimization objective. Standard training minimizes expected loss on clean data. Adversarial training minimizes worst-case loss within perturbation bounds. This shift from average-case to worst-case optimization creates more robust decision boundaries.

Implementation Approaches

Fast Gradient Sign Method (FGSM) Training generates adversarial examples efficiently by computing single-step gradients. For each training batch, compute gradients that maximize the loss. Perturb inputs in the gradient direction by a fixed magnitude. Train on both clean and perturbed examples.

FGSM training provides computational efficiency critical for large-scale training. Single-step perturbations add minimal overhead compared to standard training. However, single-step attacks produce weaker adversarial examples than multi-step methods. Models trained against FGSM may remain vulnerable to stronger attacks.

Projected Gradient Descent (PGD) Training generates stronger adversarial examples through multiple perturbation steps. Starting from clean examples, iteratively perturb in the gradient direction while projecting back to the allowed perturbation set. Multiple steps find more effective perturbations than single steps.

PGD training provides stronger robustness than FGSM training. Models trained against multi-step attacks better resist various attack types. The computational cost increases proportionally with the number of perturbation steps. Typical implementations use 7-10 steps per example.

Curriculum Adversarial Training gradually increases perturbation strength during training. Early training uses weak perturbations, enabling models to learn basic patterns. Later training uses stronger perturbations, improving robustness. This graduated approach often improves both clean accuracy and robust accuracy.

The curriculum approach balances learning robust features with maintaining performance on clean data. Starting with strong perturbations can prevent models from learning useful representations. Gradually increasing difficulty enables more effective learning.

Advanced Techniques

Ensemble Adversarial Training generates adversarial examples using multiple models rather than just the training model. Examples transfer between models with similar architectures and training data. Training on transferred adversarial examples improves robustness to transfer attacks.

This approach addresses the concern that training on self-generated adversarial examples can lead to overfitting to specific attack patterns. Using diverse adversarial sources promotes more general robustness. The technique requires maintaining multiple models, increasing computational requirements.

Unlabeled Data Augmentation leverages additional unlabeled data to improve robustness. Semi-supervised learning techniques leverage unlabeled examples alongside labeled training data. Adversarial perturbations of unlabeled data provide an additional training signal.

This approach proves particularly valuable when labeled data is scarce but unlabeled data is abundant. The additional data regularizes learning, improving both clean and robust accuracy. Consistency regularization ensures models produce similar predictions for clean and perturbed versions of unlabeled examples.

Theoretically Principled Training uses convex relaxations and verification techniques during training. Rather than generating adversarial examples through attacks, these methods compute certified worst-case bounds. Training minimizes certified worst-case loss rather than empirical worst-case loss on attack-generated examples.

These approaches provide stronger robustness guarantees than empirical adversarial training. However, computational costs typically exceed standard adversarial training. Current techniques apply primarily to smaller models and datasets. Research continues to improve scalability.

Trade-offs and Limitations

Adversarial training involves several important trade-offs:

Accuracy Trade-off: Adversarial training typically reduces accuracy on clean data while improving robust accuracy. The magnitude varies across datasets and perturbation bounds. Some applications tolerate accuracy loss better than others.

Computational Cost: Generating adversarial examples during training increases computational requirements. PGD training requires 2-3x more computation than standard training. This cost may be prohibitive for very large models or datasets.

Perturbation Bound Dependency: Robustness depends on the perturbation bound used during training. Models trained against small perturbations may not resist larger perturbations. Selecting appropriate bounds requires understanding threat models.

Attack Diversity: Training against specific attack types may not provide robustness against different attacks. Comprehensive adversarial training should include diverse perturbation strategies, further increasing computational costs.

Despite limitations, adversarial training currently provides the most effective defense against adversarial examples for many applications. Careful implementation and understanding of trade-offs enables effective deployment.

5.2 Input Validation and Sanitization

Detection-Based Defenses

Input validation detects adversarial examples before they reach models, rejecting suspicious inputs. Unlike adversarial training that hardens models, detection-based defenses operate independently of model architecture.

Statistical Testing examines input distributions for anomalies. Adversarial perturbations, while imperceptible to humans, may create statistical patterns distinguishing them from natural data. Tests examine various statistical properties identifying adversarial characteristics.

Kernel density estimation compares the test input density to the training data density. Adversarial examples often have lower density in regions where training data is concentrated. Setting density thresholds enables rejecting low-density inputs.

Dimensionality reduction techniques like PCA project inputs to lower dimensions. Adversarial perturbations may not align with the principal components of natural data. Reconstruction error after projection and reconstruction indicates potential adversarial manipulation.

Neural Network Detectors train separate models to classify inputs as clean or adversarial. Detectors train on examples labeled as clean or adversarial, learning to distinguish between them. This approach treats adversarial detection as a standard classification problem.

Detector training requires adversarial examples generated using various attacks. Detectors should train on diverse attacks to recognize multiple perturbation strategies. However, adaptive attackers might specifically craft examples evading detectors.

Feature squeezing is an input preprocessing technique that removes adversarial perturbations while preserving natural features. Color bit depth reduction and spatial smoothing eliminate small perturbations. Comparing model predictions across original and squeezed inputs reveals adversarial examples when the predictions differ significantly.

Input Transformation

Randomized Transformations apply random preprocessing to inputs before inference. Transformations like random resizing, random padding, or random quantization disrupt carefully crafted adversarial perturbations. Averaging predictions across multiple random transformations improves robustness.

This approach, called randomized smoothing, provides certified robustness guarantees under certain assumptions. Randomization creates a smoothed classifier whose predictions are provably stable within perturbation bounds. Certification requires statistical testing over multiple random transformations.

Preprocessing Pipelines apply deterministic transformations that remove adversarial perturbations. Jpeg compression, total variation minimization, and other denoising techniques can eliminate small perturbations while preserving semantic content.

Preprocessing defenses face adaptive attacks where adversaries account for transformations when generating adversarial examples. End-to-end adversarial training, including preprocessing in the computational graph, provides more robust defense than preprocessing alone.

Query Monitoring

Rate limiting restricts the number of queries per user or time period. This defense primarily addresses model extraction and privacy attacks requiring many queries. Limiting queries increases the cost of attacks without preventing single-query attacks, such as adversarial examples.

Adaptive rate limiting adjusts limits based on detected suspicious activity. Users exhibiting extraction-like behavior face stricter limits. Legitimate users with normal query patterns face minimal restrictions.

Query Pattern Analysis detects systematic exploration of model behavior. Extraction attacks often query strategically to maximize information gain. Statistical analysis identifies non-random query patterns indicating potential attacks.

Features indicating suspicious patterns include:

- High query diversity covering the input space systematically
- Queries near decision boundaries
- Repeated queries with small variations
- Queries targeting specific model behaviors

Noise Injection adds random noise to model outputs, preventing exact information extraction. Small noise additions make extraction more difficult without significantly degrading utility for legitimate users. The noise magnitude must balance security and usability.

Differential privacy provides a principled framework for output perturbation. Adding calibrated noise ensures individual queries have limited information leakage. Privacy budgets track cumulative information leakage across multiple queries.

5.3 Model Hardening Techniques

Defensive Distillation

Defensive distillation trains models using soft labels from a teacher model rather than hard labels. The soft labels encode probability distributions across classes rather than single class labels. This additional information regularizes training, producing smoother decision boundaries.

Two-Stage Process: First, train a teacher model on hard labels at an elevated temperature. Higher temperature softens the probability distribution across classes. Second, train a student model matching the teacher's soft predictions at normal temperature.

The smoothed decision boundaries make gradient-based attacks less effective. Gradients near decision boundaries have smaller magnitudes, requiring larger perturbations to cross boundaries. This increases the visibility of perturbations, making attacks easier to detect.

Defensive distillation faces limitations against strong adaptive attacks. Attackers aware of distillation can craft attacks specifically targeting distilled models. Distillation provides one layer of defense but should not serve as the sole protection.

Gradient Masking and Obfuscation

Gradient Masking techniques make gradients unavailable to attackers or uninformative to them. Non-differentiable operations in inference pipelines prevent gradient computation. Shattered gradient attacks remain possible but require more sophisticated techniques than simple gradient descent.

Approaches include:

- Quantization introducing non-differentiability
- Input transformations without clear gradients
- Stochastic prediction introducing randomness

Gradient masking provides false security if not carefully implemented. Attackers can approximate gradients using finite differences or train substitute models. Robust gradient masking must resist adaptive attacks using these techniques.

Gradient Regularization during training encourages gradients to have desired properties. Penalizing gradient magnitude near data points reduces adversarial vulnerability. Regularization terms encourage smooth loss surfaces with smaller gradients.

This approach addresses the root cause of adversarial vulnerability rather than hiding symptoms. Regularized models have fundamentally more stable decision boundaries. However, excessive regularization may reduce model capacity and accuracy.

Architectural Defenses

Defensive Layers specifically designed for robustness can be incorporated into architectures. Robust activation functions, defensive pooling layers, and certified defense layers provide robustness guarantees.

Lipschitz-constrained layers limit how much activations can change with input perturbations. Enforcing Lipschitz constraints throughout the network bounds output change for bounded input perturbations. This provides theoretical robustness guarantees.

Randomized Architectures introduce stochasticity, resisting adversarial attacks. Random feature sampling during inference makes attacks less reliable. Dropout applied at test time provides similar benefits, creating ensemble effects.

The randomness produces distributions of predictions rather than single predictions. Adversarial examples must succeed across random instantiations to be effective. This increases attack difficulty substantially.

5.4 Ensemble Methods

Diversity for Defense

Ensemble methods combine multiple models to improve robustness through diversity. Adversarial examples often transfer between similar models but transfer less effectively to diverse models. Ensembles with diverse architectures, training procedures, or data provide defense through disagreement.

Model Diversity comes from architectural differences. Combining convolutional networks, transformers, and other architectures creates ensembles where adversarial examples rarely fool all members. Each architecture has different vulnerabilities.

Training Diversity arises from different training procedures. Models trained with different hyperparameters, initializations, or data augmentations learn distinct representations. Adversarial examples crafted for one model may not affect others.

Data Diversity results from training on different data subsets or features. Models trained on different datasets learn different patterns. Perturbations effective against one model may be ineffective against models trained on different data.

Ensemble Architectures

Voting Ensembles aggregate predictions through majority voting or averaging. For classification, each model votes for a class. The ensemble prediction follows the majority or weighted vote. Adversarial examples must fool most ensemble members to succeed.

Weighted voting assigns higher weights to more reliable models. Reliability might be measured by validation accuracy, calibration quality, or adversarial robustness. Adaptive weighting adjusts based on input characteristics.

Cascade Ensembles route inputs through multiple models sequentially. Early models make initial predictions. Later models refine predictions or handle cases where early models are uncertain. This architecture enables efficiency while maintaining robustness.

Uncertain predictions trigger additional model evaluation. Clear predictions from initial models avoid the computational cost of a full ensemble. This approach balances accuracy, robustness, and computational efficiency.

Adversarially Robust Ensembles specifically optimize for robustness during ensemble construction. Rather than combining independently trained models, jointly train ensemble members to maximize robust accuracy. Training encourages diversity while ensuring individual robustness.

This approach will provide better robustness than naive ensembles. However, computational requirements increase with the ensemble size. Training multiple models jointly requires significant resources.

Limitations

Ensembles face practical limitations:

Computational Cost: Multiple model evaluations increase inference latency and resource requirements. Real-time applications may not tolerate ensemble overhead.

Adversarial Awareness: Attackers aware of ensemble composition can craft attacks targeting all members simultaneously. Black-box attacks against ensembles prove more difficult than white-box attacks.

Diminishing Returns: Adding models to ensembles provides diminishing returns in terms of robustness. Optimal ensemble size balances robustness gains against computational costs.

Despite limitations, ensembles provide meaningful improvements in robustness for many applications. Carefully designed ensembles offer strong defense against transfer attacks.

5.5 Certified Defenses

Verification-Based Approaches

Certified defenses provide mathematical guarantees that predictions remain unchanged within perturbation bounds. Unlike empirical defenses tested against specific attacks, certified defenses provide worst-case guarantees against all possible perturbations within bounds.

Interval Bound Propagation computes bounds on neuron activations throughout the network. Starting from input perturbation bounds, propagate interval bounds through each layer. Output bounds provide a certified robustness region.

This approach scales to moderately sized networks. Computational cost grows with network depth and width, but can remain tractable. However, bounds can be loose, certifying only small perturbation radii.

Linear Relaxation Methods approximate non-linear network components with linear bounds. Tighter linear bounds provide better certification radii. Various relaxation approaches trade tightness for computational efficiency.

These methods enable verifying larger networks than exact verification. However, relaxation looseness means certified regions may be smaller than true robustness regions. The certification is sound but not complete.

Complete Verification computes exact robustness regions without approximation. SMT solvers and mixed-integer programming formulate network verification as optimization problems. These approaches provide tight certificates but scale poorly to large networks.

Complete verification applies to small networks and limited perturbation types. Active research improves scalability. Current applications focus on safety-critical systems, where the benefits of verification justify the computational costs.

Randomized Smoothing

Randomized smoothing provides certified robustness through randomization. Add random noise to inputs before prediction. The smoothed classifier averages predictions across noise instantiations. Under certain noise distributions, smoothing provides certifiable robustness.

Gaussian Smoothing adds Gaussian noise to inputs. For sufficiently many noise samples, statistical testing provides certified prediction stability. The certification guarantees predictions remain constant within the certified radius with high probability.

This approach scales to large networks and datasets. Certification requires no network modifications beyond adding inference-time noise. The technique applies to any classifier. However, certification radii are often smaller than empirical robustness to gradient-based attacks.

Certification Procedure: For test input, sample many noise instantiations. Count predictions for each class. Use statistical hypothesis testing to verify that the top class remains the top class for all inputs within the certified radius.

Trade-offs

Certified defenses involve significant trade-offs:

Certification Radius: Certified robustness is typically smaller than empirical robustness. Tight certification requires conservative bounds. Practical certification radii may be quite small.

Accuracy Cost: Certified defenses often reduce clean accuracy more than empirical defenses. Strict robustness constraints limit model capacity.

Computational Overhead: Verification and certification add computational costs. Randomized smoothing requires many forward passes. Verification-based training increases training time substantially.

Perturbation Type Limitations: Most certified defenses certify specific perturbation types, such as Lp-bounded noise. Other perturbation types may not have certification guarantees.

Despite limitations, certified defenses provide value for safety-critical applications where provable guarantees justify costs. Research continues to improve certification radii and reduce computational requirements.

5.6 Runtime Monitoring and Detection

Anomaly Detection Systems

Runtime monitoring detects attacks targeting deployed models. Unlike preventive defenses that make attacks harder, monitoring enables detecting attacks that breach initial defenses. Early detection limits damage and triggers incident response.

Prediction Monitoring tracks model output distributions. Sudden changes might indicate adversarial attacks or a distribution shift. Statistical process control techniques detect changes in distribution.

Metrics to monitor include:

- Prediction confidence distributions
- Class prediction frequencies
- Entropy of prediction distributions
- Temporal prediction patterns

Significant deviations from baseline distributions trigger alerts. However, distinguishing attacks from benign distribution shifts requires careful analysis.

Activation Monitoring examines internal network activations. Adversarial examples may create unusual activation patterns. Monitoring hidden-layer activations provides visibility into the model's internals.

Autoencoders trained on clean activation patterns detect anomalous activations. High reconstruction error indicates unusual internal states potentially caused by adversarial inputs. This approach detects attacks that the model hasn't been explicitly trained against.

Gradient Monitoring analyzes gradients for suspicious patterns. Attackers often compute gradients to generate adversarial examples. Unusual gradient patterns might indicate attack preparation. However, legitimate use cases also compute gradients.

Behavioral Analysis

Query Pattern Analysis identifies systematic model exploration indicating extraction attacks. Features include:

- Query diversity and coverage
- Sequential query relationships
- Response time patterns
- Repeated similar queries

Machine learning models trained on normal and attack query patterns classify new query sequences. This meta-detection uses AI to protect AI systems.

User Behavior Profiling establishes normal behavior baselines for individual users. Deviations from established patterns indicate potential compromises. Behavioral biometrics, such as typing patterns and mouse movements, supplement traditional authentication.

This approach detects account takeover attacks where stolen credentials enable system access. Behavioral anomalies trigger additional authentication or activity restrictions.

Alerting and Response

Alert Generation requires balancing sensitivity and the false-positive rate. Overly sensitive monitoring generates alert fatigue. Insufficient sensitivity misses real attacks. Careful tuning optimizes detection performance.

Multi-level alerting provides appropriate urgency:

- Low severity alerts for minor anomalies
- Medium severity for suspicious patterns
- High severity for confirmed attacks

Alert correlation combines signals from multiple monitoring systems. Correlated alerts provide stronger evidence than individual signals.

Automated Response enables rapid reaction to detected attacks. Responses include:

- Temporarily blocking suspicious users
- Routing high-risk queries to human review
- Rolling back to previous model versions
- Activating additional defensive measures

Automation reduces response time from minutes or hours to seconds. This speed limits damage from successful attacks.

Human Review validates automated detections and handles complex cases. Security operations teams investigate alerts, determine root causes, and implement appropriate responses. Human judgment handles nuanced situations that automation cannot.

5.7 Defense Against Specific Attack Types

Data Poisoning Defenses

Data Validation examines training data before use. Techniques include:

- Provenance verification ensuring data origins
- Statistical outlier detection, identifying anomalies
- Label consistency checking across multiple annotators
- Clustering analysis revealing suspicious groupings

Validation cannot catch all of the poisoning, especially sophisticated clean-label attacks. Defense requires multiple layers.

Robust Training Algorithms tolerate limited corruption in training data. Approaches include:

- Trimmed loss functions discarding the worst-performing examples
- Sample reweighting, down-weighting suspicious examples
- Outlier-robust optimization, like median-based methods

These algorithms assume corruption affects only a minority of training data. Severe poisoning requires additional defenses.

Backdoor Detection searches for triggers in trained models. Techniques include:

- Reverse engineering potential triggers
- Activation clustering identifying backdoor-specific patterns
- Fine-tuning analysis detecting embedded behaviors

Detection enables removing backdoors before deployment. However, determined attackers create stealthy backdoors that resist detection.

Model Extraction Defenses

Query Limiting restricts query volume per user. Rate limits increase extraction costs by requiring more time or additional accounts. However, determined attackers may be willing to accept increased costs.

Response perturbation adds noise to predictions, reducing extraction accuracy. Small perturbations hinder extraction without significantly impacting legitimate use. Differential privacy provides principled perturbation.

Watermarking embeds signatures in model behavior, enabling the detection of extracted models. Watermarks should be difficult to remove while not affecting normal performance. Detecting watermarks in suspect models provides evidence of theft.

Privacy Attack Defenses

Differential Privacy during training limits memorization. Adding calibrated noise prevents models from memorizing individual training examples. This provides mathematical privacy guarantees.

Federated Learning keeps training data distributed. Models train on local data without centralization. Only model updates transfer, not raw data. This architectural approach fundamentally limits data exposure.

Aggregation combines information across many users before release. Statistical databases provide query results about groups rather than individuals. Aggregation protects individual privacy while enabling useful analysis.

5.8 Defense Evaluation and Testing

Adversarial Robustness Metrics

Effective defense requires measuring robustness quantitatively. Several metrics assess adversarial robustness:

Robust Accuracy measures accuracy on adversarial examples. For perturbation bound epsilon, robust accuracy is the fraction of examples classified correctly under the worst-case perturbation within epsilon. This directly measures defense effectiveness.

Certified Robust Accuracy measures accuracy within certified robustness regions. Only examples with certified regions larger than epsilon count as robust. This provides conservative robustness estimates with guarantees.

Attack Success Rate measures the fraction of clean examples successfully perturbed into adversarial examples. Lower success rates indicate stronger defenses. This metric depends on attack strength and budget.

Perturbation Budget measures the minimum perturbation magnitude needed to fool models. Larger required perturbations indicate more robust models. Different perturbation metrics (L2, L-infinity, perceptual) provide different perspectives.

Testing Methodology

White-Box Testing provides attackers with full access to the model. This worst-case testing reveals fundamental robustness. Passing white-box tests provides strong confidence in the effectiveness of the defense. Testing should employ multiple attack algorithms:

- Fast gradient sign method
- Projected gradient descent with multiple steps

- Carlini-Wagner optimization-based attacks
- Adaptive attacks aware of specific defenses

Black-Box Testing restricts attackers to query access. This realistic scenario tests the practical difficulty of an attack. Query budgets simulate resource constraints that attackers face.

Black-box testing should include:

- Transfer attacks using surrogate models
- Query-based attacks estimating gradients
- Genetic algorithms exploring input space

Red Team Exercises involve security experts attacking systems creatively. Human attackers think beyond automated attack algorithms. Red teams combine multiple techniques and exploit unexpected vulnerabilities.

Effective red teaming requires:

- Adversarial mindset seeking to break systems
- Deep technical knowledge of AI and security
- Access to system internals for thorough testing
- Clear rules of engagement and reporting

Continuous Evaluation

Defense effectiveness must be monitored continuously after deployment. Attackers adapt to deployed defenses. New attack techniques emerge. Regular reevaluation ensures defenses remain effective.

Regression Testing verifies defenses don't degrade during model updates. Each new model version should undergo adversarial testing before deployment. Automated testing pipelines enable continuous validation of defenses.

Threat Intelligence tracks emerging attack techniques. Security research continually develops novel attacks. Monitoring research enables proactively testing defenses against new threats before attackers weaponize them.

Bug Bounty Programs incentivize external researchers to find vulnerabilities. Paying rewards for discovered weaknesses encourages responsible disclosure. Bounties should cover adversarial examples, model extraction, privacy attacks, and other AI-specific vulnerabilities.

5.9 Incident Response for AI Systems

Preparation

Effective incident response requires preparation before incidents occur. Organizations should establish:

Response Teams with clearly defined roles:

- Incident commander coordinating response
- Technical investigators analyzing attacks
- Communications lead managing internal and external communications
- Legal counsel advising on regulatory obligations
- Business stakeholders assessing impact

Cross-functional teams ensure a comprehensive response addressing technical, legal, and business dimensions.

Response Procedures documenting steps for common scenarios:

- Adversarial example detection and mitigation
- Data poisoning discovery and remediation
- Model extraction, detection, and legal action
- Privacy breach notification and remediation

Documented procedures enable rapid, consistent response under pressure.

Communication Channels enabling rapid team coordination:

- Primary communication platform
- Backup communication for infrastructure failures
- Escalation procedures for severe incidents
- Stakeholder notification workflows

Reliable communications prove critical during high-stress incident response.

Detection and Analysis

Initial Detection comes from monitoring systems or external reports. Alerts should provide sufficient context for initial assessment. Triage determines incident severity and appropriate response level.

Investigation examines evidence determining:

- Attack vector and methodology
- Affected systems and data
- Attack timeline and duration
- Attacker identity, if possible

Forensic analysis preserves evidence supporting investigation and potential legal action.

Containment and Recovery

Immediate Containment limits ongoing damage:

- Blocking attacker access
- Isolating affected systems
- Rolling back to known-good configurations
- Activating additional defenses

Quick containment prevents damage escalation.

Eradication removes attack artifacts and vulnerabilities:

- Removing backdoors from models
- Cleaning poisoned training data
- Patching exploited vulnerabilities
- Updating defensive measures

Thorough eradication prevents attack recurrence.

Recovery restores normal operations:

- Retraining models on validated clean data
- Restoring from backups if necessary
- Validating system integrity before production
- Gradual restoration monitoring for issues

Careful recovery ensures systems are genuinely secure before resuming operations.

Post-Incident Activities

Lessons Learned analyzes incidents to improve future response:

- How was the attack successful?
- What detection mechanisms worked or failed?
- How could the response improve?
- What systemic issues enabled the attack?

Blameless retrospectives focus on systemic improvements rather than individual mistakes.

Documentation records incident details:

- Attack timeline and methodology
- Detection and response actions
- Impact assessment
- Remediation measures

Documentation supports regulatory reporting, insurance claims, and organizational learning.

Preventive Measures implement improvements:

- Deploying additional defenses
- Updating monitoring systems
- Improving detection capabilities
- Training staff on new threats

Converting lessons learned into concrete improvements prevents similar incidents.

Chapter Summary

This chapter provided comprehensive guidance for building robust AI system defenses:

Adversarial Training: Training on adversarial examples improves robustness by teaching models to handle perturbed inputs. Techniques range from efficient FGSM training to comprehensive PGD training. Trade-offs include reduced clean accuracy and increased computational costs.

Input Validation: Detection-based defenses identify adversarial inputs before they reach models. Statistical testing, neural network detectors, and transformation-based approaches provide various detection capabilities. Query monitoring addresses extraction and privacy attacks.

Model Hardening: Defensive distillation, gradient masking, and architectural modifications improve the inherent robustness of models. These techniques complement training-based defenses.

Ensemble Methods: Combining diverse models provides defense through disagreement. Adversarial examples that fool one model often fail against ensemble members with different architectures or training.

Certified Defenses: Verification-based approaches and randomized smoothing provide mathematical guarantees of robustness. Certifications assure predictions remain stable within perturbation bounds.

Runtime Monitoring: Anomaly detection, behavioral analysis, and alerting systems detect attacks targeting deployed models. Early detection enables rapid response, limiting damage.

Specific Attack Defenses: Specialized techniques address data poisoning, model extraction, and privacy attacks. Layered defenses across the AI lifecycle provide comprehensive protection.

Evaluation and Testing: Quantitative metrics and comprehensive testing methodologies assess defense effectiveness. Continuous evaluation ensures defenses remain effective as threats evolve.

Incident Response: Preparation, detection, containment, recovery, and post-incident analysis enable effective response to successful attacks. Documented procedures and trained teams minimize damage.

Effective defense requires combining multiple complementary techniques. No single defense provides complete protection. Layered approaches addressing different attack vectors create robust systems.

Key Takeaways

1. Adversarial training provides the most effective empirical defense against adversarial examples but involves trade-offs between clean accuracy and robust accuracy.

2. Detection-based defenses complement robustness improvements by identifying attacks that breach initial defenses. Layered detection and prevention provide defense-in-depth.

3. Ensemble methods exploit diversity to improve robustness. Attacks that transfer to one model often fail against models with different architectures or training.

4. Certified defenses provide mathematical guarantees, but currently certify smaller perturbation radii than empirical defenses achieve. They prove most valuable for safety-critical applications.

5. Runtime monitoring enables detecting attacks targeting deployed systems. Early detection limits damage and triggers incident response.

6. Defense effectiveness requires continuous evaluation. New attacks emerge constantly. Regular testing ensures defenses remain effective against evolving threats.

7. Comprehensive defense addresses multiple attack types across the AI lifecycle. Data poisoning, adversarial examples, model extraction, and privacy attacks each require specific defensive measures.

8. Incident response preparation proves critical for minimizing damage when attacks succeed. Documented procedures and trained teams enable rapid, effective response.

Reflection Questions

1. Consider deploying an autonomous vehicle vision system. What combination of defensive techniques would you prioritize, and how would you justify the trade-offs to stakeholders?

2. If adversarial training reduces clean accuracy by 5% while improving robust accuracy by 30%, how do you determine whether this trade-off is acceptable? What factors inform this decision?

3. Compare the value of certified defenses providing small certified radii versus empirical defenses providing larger uncertified robustness. When does each approach make sense?

4. How would you design a monitoring system that detects model extraction attacks without creating excessive false positives from legitimate heavy users?

5. If your organization experiences a data poisoning incident, what steps would you take to determine which training data is corrupted and whether deployed models contain backdoors?

6. Consider an ensemble of five models where three use convolutional architectures and two use transformers. How does this composition affect robustness against transfer attacks compared to an ensemble of five identical-architecture models?

7. What tensions exist between transparency requirements that enable accountability and security concerns that favor opacity in defensive mechanisms? How do you navigate these tensions for specific deployment contexts?

6

Industry-Specific AI Security Implementation

Learning Objectives

By the end of this chapter, you will:

- Understand unique security challenges facing AI systems in healthcare, finance, manufacturing, retail, and transportation
- Apply industry-specific regulatory requirements to AI security implementations
- Implement sector-appropriate threat models addressing industry-specific adversaries
- Design security architectures meeting industry compliance standards
- Balance security requirements with operational constraints in different sectors
- Navigate industry-specific privacy and ethical considerations
- Deploy monitoring systems tailored to sector-specific threats

Introduction: Context-Dependent Security

AI security principles apply universally, but implementation details depend heavily on industry context. Healthcare AI faces different threats than financial AI. Manufacturing systems operate under different constraints than retail systems. Regulatory requirements, threat actors, risk tolerances, and operational constraints vary dramatically across sectors.

This chapter explores AI security implementation across major industries. We examine sector-specific threats, regulatory requirements, implementation challenges, and proven solutions. The goal is to translate general security principles into concrete practices for specific contexts.

Each industry section follows a consistent structure. We begin by characterizing the sector's AI applications and unique security challenges. We then examine regulatory frameworks and compliance requirements. Next, we present threat models identifying sector-specific adversaries and attack vectors. Finally, we provide implementation guidance with proven architectures and practices.

The industries covered represent major AI adopters facing significant security challenges. However, principles and practices discussed generalize to other sectors. Readers can adapt approaches to their specific contexts by understanding how industry characteristics shape security requirements.

6.1 Healthcare

Industry Characteristics

Healthcare organizations deploy AI for diagnostics, treatment planning, drug discovery, patient monitoring, and administrative tasks. These applications process highly sensitive personal health information protected by extensive regulations. Patient safety concerns create low tolerance for errors. Medical device regulations add complexity to AI deployment.

Healthcare AI operates in environments where:

- Data sensitivity is extremely high with serious privacy implications
- Safety criticality means errors can directly harm patients
- Regulatory scrutiny is intense, with significant penalties for violations
- System availability requirements are stringent for emergency care
- Long operational lifetimes mean systems must remain secure for years

Threat Landscape

Adversaries targeting healthcare AI include:

Cybercriminals seek patient data for identity theft and fraud. Medical records fetch high prices on black markets. Ransomware attacks disrupt healthcare operations while demanding payment.

Nation-State Actors target research data and intellectual property. Pharmaceutical research and genomic data are valuable sources of intelligence. Advanced persistent threats compromise systems for long-term espionage.

Insiders with legitimate access may misuse systems. Curious employees might access celebrity medical records. Malicious insiders could manipulate diagnostic systems for personal gain or harm.

Adversarial Patients might manipulate diagnostic systems to obtain desired diagnoses. Drug seekers might game pain assessment algorithms. Insurance fraudsters might manipulate systems to increase reimbursements.

Attack Vectors specific to healthcare AI:

Training Data Poisoning could compromise diagnostic accuracy. Adversaries might inject mislabeled examples, causing systematic misdiagnosis. Subtle poisoning might target specific patient populations.

Model Extraction enables competitors to replicate proprietary diagnostic algorithms. Systematic querying of diagnostic APIs can reconstruct model functionality.

Privacy Attacks extract sensitive patient information from trained models. Membership inference reveals whether specific patients contributed to training data. Model inversion reconstructs patient records from model parameters.

Adversarial Examples could cause misdiagnosis. Subtle perturbations in medical images might hide tumors or lead to false positives. Physical adversarial attacks could manipulate sensor data from wearable devices.

Regulatory Requirements

HIPAA (Health Insurance Portability and Accountability Act) establishes privacy and security requirements for protected health information:

The Privacy Rule limits the use and disclosure of health information. AI systems must process the minimum necessary information. Patient consent requirements affect the collection of training data.

Security Rule mandates administrative, physical, and technical safeguards. Access controls, audit logging, encryption, and integrity controls protect electronic health information.

The Breach Notification Rule requires reporting compromises of unsecured health information. Organizations must notify affected individuals, HHS, and, if applicable, the media when breaches occur.

FDA Oversight applies to AI-enabled medical devices:

Software as Medical Device (SaMD) regulations establish safety and effectiveness requirements. AI systems that diagnose disease or guide treatment face extensive validation requirements.

Predetermined Change Control Plans enable updating AI systems without full reapproval. Organizations must demonstrate that changes remain within validated safe envelopes.

Post-Market Surveillance requires ongoing monitoring of deployed medical devices. Adverse event reporting captures problems occurring in real-world use.

GDPR and International Regulations affect multinational healthcare organizations. European health data processing is subject to additional privacy requirements. Cross-border data transfers require appropriate safeguards.

Implementation Guidance

Data Security Architecture:

De-identification and Anonymization protect patient privacy during AI development. Remove direct identifiers like names and medical record numbers. Apply k-anonymity, l-diversity, or differential privacy for stronger protection.

However, de-identification faces challenges. Rare medical conditions pose a risk of re-identification even after removing direct identifiers. Genomic data is inherently identifying. Balance privacy protection with utility for medical AI.

Federated Learning enables collaborative research without centralizing sensitive data. Hospitals train models on local data and share only model updates. Secure aggregation prevents coordinators from seeing individual hospital updates.

This approach maintains data locality, addressing privacy and regulatory concerns. However, Byzantine-robust aggregation becomes critical.

Malicious participants could poison global models through corrupted updates.

Homomorphic Encryption enables processing encrypted medical data. Diagnostic systems can analyze encrypted patient information, producing encrypted results that only patients can decrypt. Current implementations face performance challenges but continue improving.

Model Development Best Practices:

Diverse Training Data prevents bias affecting diagnosis quality. Ensure training data represents diverse patient populations across age, sex, ethnicity, and geography. Evaluate model performance separately for demographic subgroups.

Historical medical data reflects biases in past care. Carefully examine training data for systematic biases. Consider rebalancing or reweighting to promote equitable performance.

Adversarial Robustness proves critical for patient safety. Medical AI must resist adversarial examples that could cause misdiagnosis. Test robustness using medical domain expertise to generate realistic adversarial scenarios.

Physical adversarial attacks pose particular concern. Medical imaging equipment could be tampered with. Ensure end-to-end integrity from sensors through inference.

Explainability helps clinicians trust and verify AI recommendations. Provide explanations indicating which image regions influenced the diagnosis. Enable clinicians to understand and validate model reasoning. However, explanations must be accurate. Misleading explanations create false confidence. Validate that the explanations accurately reflect the model's behavior.

Deployment Architecture:

Human-in-the-Loop systems keep clinicians in decision loops. AI provides recommendations that clinicians review before acting. This approach maintains human oversight while benefiting from AI capabilities.

Define clear protocols for human review. Specify which cases require additional scrutiny. Train clinicians to critically evaluate AI recommendations.

Safety Monitoring detects potential harms from deployed systems. Track diagnostic accuracy on ongoing cases with confirmed diagnoses. Monitor for systematic errors affecting specific patient populations.

Adverse event reporting captures problems occurring in practice. Clear reporting procedures enable rapid identification of safety issues.

Version Control and Rollback enable rapid response to discovered problems. Maintain previous model versions to enable quick rollbacks. Test new versions thoroughly before deployment.

Document model changes and their validation. Regulatory submissions may require demonstrating the safety of updates.

Case Study: Diagnostic AI Bias

A widely deployed sepsis prediction algorithm showed significant bias across racial groups. The system used fewer predictors for Black patients compared to white patients with similar health status, resulting in delayed interventions.

Root Cause: Training data reflected historical disparities in care access and intensity. The model learned to predict sepsis risk based on historical treatment patterns rather than actual clinical need.

Impact: Thousands of patients potentially received delayed care due to systematic underestimation of risk for Black patients. This bias violated fairness principles and potentially caused patient harm.

Remediation: The healthcare system implemented comprehensive bias audits across all predictive algorithms. They retrained models using debiased objectives and validated performance across demographic groups. Additional review processes now catch potential biases before deployment.

Lessons: Historical medical data contains biases that AI systems can amplify. Fairness evaluation across patient demographics must be standard practice. Clinical validation should explicitly test for disparate impact.

6.2 Financial Services

Industry Characteristics

Financial institutions deploy AI for fraud detection, credit scoring, algorithmic trading, customer service, and risk management. These applications involve large financial stakes and extensive regulation. Real-time processing requirements constrain acceptable computational overhead. An adversarial environment means determined attackers continuously probe systems.

Financial AI operates where:

- Adversarial pressure is intense with significant financial motivation
- Real-time requirements limit acceptable processing delays
- Regulatory compliance is mandatory with severe penalties
- Accuracy requirements are high, as errors have a direct financial impact
- Explainability demands exist for adverse decisions

Threat Landscape

Adversaries:

Organized Criminals target financial systems for fraud and theft. Credit card fraud, money laundering, and identity theft represent major threats. Criminal organizations operate sophisticated operations with technical capabilities.

Nation-State Actors conduct espionage and economic warfare. State-sponsored attacks target trading algorithms, economic intelligence, and financial infrastructure. These adversaries possess significant resources and patience.

Insider Threats with system access pose significant risks. Rogue traders might manipulate risk models. Corrupt employees might leak customer data. Insider threats combine high access with motivation.

Competitors may engage in industrial espionage. Proprietary trading algorithms represent valuable intellectual property. Model extraction enables competitors to replicate capabilities without development investment.

Attack Vectors:

Adversarial Fraud crafts transactions evading fraud detection. Attackers test fraud-detection boundaries, finding transactions that are incorrectly classified as legitimate. Adaptive adversaries evolve techniques as defenses improve.

Model Manipulation targets credit scoring and risk models. Applicants' game applications appear more creditworthy. Attackers might inject false data into training sets, thereby biasing the model's behavior.

Algorithmic Market Manipulation exploits trading algorithms. Spoofing, layering, and other manipulative techniques trigger algorithms into unfavorable trades. High-frequency trading creates opportunities for sophisticated attacks.

Privacy Attacks extract customer financial information. Membership inference determines whether individuals appear in training data. Model inversion reconstructs transaction patterns from model behavior.

Regulatory Requirements

Fair Lending Laws prohibit discrimination in credit decisions:

The Equal Credit Opportunity Act (ECOA) prohibits discrimination based on protected characteristics. Credit models must not systematically disadvantage protected groups. Adverse action notices must explain credit denials.

The Fair Housing Act extends protection to housing-related credit. Mortgage lending models face scrutiny for discriminatory impacts. Disparate impact on protected groups violates fair housing requirements even without intent.

Anti-Money Laundering (AML) Regulations require detecting and reporting suspicious activities:

The Bank Secrecy Act mandates transaction monitoring and suspicious activity reporting. AI systems must identify potentially criminal transactions while minimizing false positives affecting legitimate customers.

Know Your Customer (KYC) requirements verify customer identities and assess risk. AI-powered identity verification must balance fraud prevention with customer experience.

Market Manipulation Rules prohibit deceptive trading practices:

Securities regulations prohibit spoofing, layering, and other manipulative techniques. Trading algorithms must operate within regulatory bounds. Demonstrating algorithmic fairness and proper controls proves challenging.

GDPR and Privacy Regulations affect customer data processing: Credit scoring using personal data requires a legal basis. Data minimization and purpose limitation constrain data collection. Right to explanation creates transparency requirements for automated credit decisions.

Implementation Guidance

Fraud Detection Architecture:

Ensemble Models improve detection while reducing false positives. Combine rule-based systems, statistical models, and neural networks. Diversity in detection approaches catches different fraud types.

Multiple models operating independently can prevent attackers from optimizing fraud to evade all detectors simultaneously. Voting or a weighted combination produces final decisions.

Adversarial Training hardens models against adversarial fraud. Train on both legitimate transactions and adversarial examples that simulate fraudulent attempts. Continuously update adversarial examples as attack techniques evolve.

This arms race requires ongoing vigilance. Adversaries adapt to deployed defenses. Regular model retraining with fresh adversarial examples maintains effectiveness.

Behavioral Biometrics provides continuous authentication. Analyze typing patterns, mouse movements, and device handling. Unusual behavioral patterns trigger additional verification.

This approach detects account takeover even with compromised credentials. Behavioral profiles are difficult for attackers to replicate convincingly.

Credit Scoring Best Practices:

Fairness Auditing ensures equitable treatment across demographic groups. Test models for disparate impact on protected groups. Implement debiasing techniques when disparate impact is detected without a legitimate business justification.

Document fairness testing thoroughly. Regulatory examinations increasingly scrutinize algorithmic fairness. Proactive auditing demonstrates compliance commitment.

Explainability enables adverse action notices and appeals. Provide applicants with factors influencing credit decisions. Explanations must be accurate, specific, and actionable.

Use techniques like SHAP or LIME to generate feature-based explanations. Validate that explanations genuinely reflect model behavior rather than providing misleading post-hoc rationalizations.

Alternative Data improves credit access but requires careful validation. Non-traditional data, such as utility payments or rental history, can improve creditworthiness assessment. However, ensure alternative data doesn't introduce new biases or violate privacy.

Trading Algorithm Security:

Market Manipulation Detection prevents regulatory violations. Monitor algorithms for behavior resembling spoofing, layering, or wash trading. Automated circuit breakers halt trading when suspicious patterns emerge.

Pre-deployment testing validates that algorithms operate within regulatory bounds. Backtesting on historical data and forward testing in simulation environments catch potential issues before live deployment.

Kill Switches enable rapid response to malfunctioning algorithms. Automated monitoring detects abnormal behavior, triggering automatic suspension. Human oversight provides final authority over algorithm activation.

Document all algorithm changes and their validation. Regulatory inquiries following market events require demonstrating proper controls and oversight.

Case Study: Flash Crash Investigation

A 2010 "Flash Crash" saw markets plunge and recover within minutes, partly attributed to algorithmic trading. Investigations revealed cascading algorithmic interactions that created unintended feedback loops.

Root Cause: Algorithms reacting to price movements triggered other algorithms, creating a positive feedback loop. No single algorithm behaved incorrectly, but their interactions created systemic instability.

Response: Regulators implemented circuit breakers and position limits. Trading firms enhanced pre-deployment testing and monitoring. The industry developed better practices for analyzing algorithmic interactions.

Lessons: AI systems operating in shared environments can exhibit emergent behavior. Testing individual system correctness proves insufficient. Interaction effects require analysis and mitigation.

6.3 Manufacturing and Industrial IoT

Industry Characteristics

Manufacturing organizations deploy AI for predictive maintenance, quality control, supply chain optimization, and autonomous systems.

Industrial IoT sensors provide data for AI analysis. Real-time control systems integrate AI into production processes.

Manufacturing AI operates where:

- Physical safety is paramount as failures can injure workers
- Operational continuity is critical with downtime costs
- Equipment lifetimes span decades, requiring long-term security
- Resource constraints affect edge devices and sensors
- Supply chain complexity introduces many potential compromise points

Threat Landscape

Adversaries:

Nation-State Actors target critical infrastructure and intellectual property. Industrial espionage steals manufacturing processes and product designs. Infrastructure attacks disrupt production, causing economic damage.

Competitors seek proprietary manufacturing knowledge. Production optimization algorithms represent competitive advantages. Model extraction enables competitors to replicate operational efficiencies.

Insiders with physical access can compromise systems. Disgruntled employees might sabotage production. Contractors might plant backdoors in industrial control systems.

Ransomware Groups target manufacturers, knowing production downtime costs. Encrypting production systems or threatening to damage equipment creates leverage for ransom demands.

Attack Vectors:

Sensor Spoofing manipulates the data fed to AI systems. False sensor readings can lead to incorrect predictions or decisions. Physical access to sensors enables injection attacks.

Adversarial Attacks on Vision Systems compromise quality control. Subtle product perturbations might evade defect detection. This enables shipping defective products or concealing sabotage.

Supply Chain Attacks compromise equipment or software. Malicious components embedded in industrial IoT devices provide persistent access. Compromised firmware updates inject backdoors.

Model Poisoning in predictive maintenance could delay critical repairs. Manipulating training data might cause systems to ignore failure indicators. Unexpected equipment failures result from compromised predictions.

Regulatory Requirements

Safety Regulations vary by industry:

OSHA (Occupational Safety and Health Administration) sets workplace safety standards. AI systems affecting worker safety face regulatory scrutiny. Demonstrating safe operation requires extensive testing and validation.

Industry-specific standards, such as automotive functional safety (ISO 26262) or machinery safety (IEC 61508), establish requirements. AI systems must demonstrate compliance with applicable standards.

Cybersecurity Standards:

The NIST Cybersecurity Framework provides guidelines for protecting critical infrastructure. Many industries adopt the NIST framework for systematic security management.

IEC 62443 establishes security standards for industrial automation and control systems. Segmentation, access control, and monitoring requirements apply to AI-enabled industrial systems.

Product Security Standards:

UL 2900 series covers software cybersecurity for network-connectable products. Connected manufacturing equipment should undergo security evaluation and certification.

Implementation Guidance

Predictive Maintenance Security:

Anomaly Detection identifies unusual equipment behavior that may indicate attacks. Distinguish between legitimate anomalies signaling equipment issues and malicious anomalies indicating compromise.

Baseline normal behavior during commissioning. Use statistical process control to detect deviations from baselines. Investigate unusual patterns before acting on predictions.

Sensor Validation verifies sensor data integrity. Multiple sensors measuring related quantities enable cross-validation. Physics-based models predict expected sensor relationships. Violations indicate sensor compromise or equipment issues.

Cryptographic authentication of sensor data prevents injection attacks. Digital signatures prove that the data originated from legitimate sensors. However, resource-constrained devices may struggle with cryptographic overhead.

Secure Updates enable patching vulnerabilities without production disruption. Digitally signed updates prevent malicious firmware injection. Staged rollouts enable problems to be detected before full deployment.

However, the operational lifetimes of equipment complicate patching. Legacy systems may lack update mechanisms. Strategies must address securing systems designed before modern security practices emerged.

Quality Control AI Security:

Adversarial Robustness prevents evasion of defect detection. Test vision systems against adversarial examples designed to hide defects. Physical adversarial attacks on production lines require defense.

Multiple independent inspection systems provide defense through diversity. Defects must evade all systems simultaneously to pass inspection. However, this increases inspection costs and complexity.

Human Verification maintains oversight of automated inspection. Sample products undergo human inspection to validate AI decisions. Unexpected defect patterns trigger expanded human review.

Supply Chain Security:

Vendor Assessment evaluates suppliers' security practices. Require security certifications from component vendors. Audit vendor security for high-risk components.

Bill of Materials Tracking maintains an inventory of all system components. Know exactly what hardware and software compose each system. This enables targeted response when component vulnerabilities are discovered.

Secure Provisioning establishes trust in newly deployed devices. Factory initialization establishes cryptographic identities. Secure boot ensures only authorized software executes.

Case Study: Industrial Control System Compromise

A steel mill experienced unusual furnace behavior traced to compromised temperature sensors feeding AI control systems. Attackers manipulated readings, causing unsafe operating conditions.

Attack Path: Internet-facing administrative interface with weak authentication provided initial access. Lateral movement reached industrial network segments. Persistent access enabled long-term manipulation of sensor data.

Impact: Unsafe furnace operation posed a risk of equipment damage and worker injury. Identifying the compromise took weeks as unusual behavior was initially attributed to equipment issues rather than attacks.

Remediation: Network segmentation of isolated industrial control systems. Enhanced monitoring detected anomalous sensor patterns. Multiple independent sensors enable cross-validation and detect manipulation.

Lessons: Physical safety systems require a defense-in-depth approach. Network segmentation prevents IT compromises from reaching OT systems. Physics-based validation catches sensor manipulation.

6.4 Retail and E-Commerce

Industry Characteristics

Retailers deploy AI for recommendation systems, dynamic pricing, inventory management, customer service chatbots, and fraud detection. These systems directly impact customer experience and business revenue. High transaction volumes require efficient real-time processing.

Retail AI operates where:

- Customer experience directly affects business success
- Processing efficiency matters for user-facing systems
- Privacy concerns affect customer trust and loyalty
- Seasonal demand variations create operational challenges
- Competition is intense with low customer switching costs

Threat Landscape

Adversaries:

Fraudsters exploit payment systems and promotions. Credit card fraud, return fraud, and coupon abuse represent major concerns. Organized retail crime uses sophisticated techniques.

Competitors seek pricing algorithms and customer intelligence. Dynamic pricing strategies represent competitive advantages. Customer behavior models inform marketing and operations.

Scalpers and Bots manipulate inventory systems. Automated purchasing depletes the limited inventory. Scalpers resell high-demand products at a markup. This frustrates legitimate customers and damages brand reputation.

Privacy Advocates scrutinize data collection and use. Extensive behavioral tracking enables personalization but raises privacy concerns. Inadequate privacy protection risks regulatory penalties and reputation damage.

Attack Vectors:

Recommendation System Manipulation pushes specific products. Attackers use game recommendation algorithms to promote their products or demote competitors. Fake reviews and manipulated user behavior poison recommendation models.

Price Manipulation exploits dynamic pricing algorithms. Competitors might probe pricing to reverse-engineer algorithms. Coordinated price-checking behavior could manipulate prices, benefiting attackers.

Inventory Gaming uses bots to deplete stock. Automated purchasing at scale acquires the entire inventory of limited products. This enables scalping while frustrating legitimate customers.

Privacy Attacks extract customer information from recommendation models. Membership inference determines shopping behaviors. Model inversion reconstructs purchase histories.

Implementation Guidance

Recommendation System Security:

Robust Training resists manipulation through fake reviews and shill accounts. Statistical outlier detection identifies suspicious review patterns. Graph analysis detects coordinated manipulation campaigns.

Downweight reviews from accounts with suspicious characteristics. New accounts, accounts with unusual review patterns, or accounts clustered in social graphs might indicate manipulation attempts.

Diversity in Recommendations prevents over-optimization for manipulated signals. Ensuring diverse recommendations reduces the impact. Even if attackers boost specific products, diverse recommendations limit their promotion.

Explainability enables users to understand recommendations. Showing why products were recommended builds trust. Users can identify and report inappropriate recommendations.

Dynamic Pricing Security:

Rate limiting prevents price discovery through systematic probing. Limit the number of price checks per user and time period. Detect automated price-checking behavior blocking bots.

Obfuscation adds noise to published prices. Small random price variations complicate algorithm reverse-engineering. However, this must balance with customer trust and legal requirements for honest pricing.

Monitoring detects unusual price patterns that may indicate algorithmic compromise or gaming. Alert on unexpected price volatility or patterns inconsistent with demand and competition.

Bot Detection and Mitigation:

Behavioral Analysis distinguishes human users from bots. Analyze mouse movements, typing patterns, and browsing behaviors. Humans exhibit natural variations that bots struggle to replicate convincingly.

Challenge-Response blocks automated access. CAPTCHA, device fingerprinting, and rate limiting raise bot costs. However, these may frustrate legitimate users, requiring careful implementation.

Inventory Protection reserves stock for likely legitimate purchasers. Risk-based allocation considers account history and purchase patterns. High-risk purchases face additional verification.

Privacy-Preserving Analytics:

Differential Privacy protects customer information in analytics. Add calibrated noise to queries to prevent inference of individual behavior. This enables aggregate analysis while protecting individual privacy.

Federated Analytics analyzes behavior without centralizing sensitive data. Perform computations locally on customer devices, reporting only aggregated statistics. This approach addresses privacy while enabling personalization.

Data Minimization collects only necessary information. Clear data retention policies delete historical data after it loses utility. This limits the impact of breaches and demonstrates a commitment to privacy.

Case Study: Recommendation System Gaming

An online marketplace discovered systematic manipulation of its recommendation algorithm. Coordinated groups created fake accounts, generating fraudulent positive reviews and purchases for specific products while attacking competitors with negative reviews.

Detection: Anomaly detection identified products with unusual review velocity and patterns. Graph analysis revealed clustered accounts engaging in coordinated behavior.

Impact: Manipulated products received prominent recommendations despite questionable quality. Legitimate products were unfairly downranked. Customer trust in recommendations eroded.

Response: Enhanced review validation downweights suspicious reviews. Graph-based fraud detection identifies manipulation networks. Regular audits check for recommendation gaming.

Lessons: User-generated signals are vulnerable to manipulation. Adversarial data poisoning extends beyond model training to ongoing user interactions. Robust algorithms must resist manipulation in production.

6.5 Transportation and Autonomous Systems

Industry Characteristics

Transportation industries deploy AI for autonomous vehicles, traffic management, route optimization, and predictive maintenance. Safety-critical applications require extremely high reliability. Real-time decision-making operates under strict latency constraints. Physical environments create opportunities for attack and its consequences.

Transportation AI operates where:

- Safety is paramount with the potential loss of life
- Real-time constraints require rapid decision-making
- Physical environment provides attack vectors
- Mixed autonomy creates human-AI interaction challenges
- Infrastructure interdependencies create systemic risks

Threat Landscape

Adversaries:

Malicious Actors seeking to cause harm could target vehicles and infrastructure. Terrorist attacks might exploit autonomous systems. Random attackers might vandalize or tamper for entertainment.

Nation-state actors may target transportation infrastructure in conflict scenarios. Disrupting logistics or public transit creates strategic advantages. Critical infrastructure attacks represent potential warfare tactics.

Researchers investigating vulnerabilities might inadvertently create public risks. Published attacks on autonomous vehicles could enable copycat attacks. Responsible disclosure becomes critical but challenging.

Attack Vectors:

Sensor Spoofing manipulates perception systems. GPS spoofing redirects autonomous vehicles. Lidar spoofing creates phantom obstacles or hides real ones. Camera-based perception faces adversarial example attacks.

Adversarial Physical Objects exploit vision systems. Modified road signs fool traffic sign recognition. Adversarial patterns on roads or objects cause misclassification. Physical world constraints make attacks detectable but enable persistent presence.

V2V/V2I Communication Attacks compromise vehicle-to-vehicle and vehicle-to-infrastructure communication. False messages could cause unnecessary braking or route changes. Denial-of-service prevents receiving legitimate safety messages.

Model Extraction reveals proprietary autonomous driving algorithms. Systematic probing of behavior enables inferring decision logic. Competitors could replicate capabilities without development investment.

Regulatory Requirements

Safety Standards:

ISO 26262 (Functional Safety for Road Vehicles) establishes requirements for automotive systems. Achieving Automotive Safety Integrity Level (ASIL) ratings requires demonstrating systematic safety practices.

SOTIF (Safety of the Intended Functionality) addresses limitations of automated systems. Beyond random hardware failures, SOTIF requires addressing systematic design limitations and environmental triggers.

Testing and Validation:

NHTSA Guidance provides voluntary best practices for autonomous vehicles. Extensive testing, cybersecurity practices, and post-crash behavior requirements inform development.

State Regulations vary regarding autonomous vehicle testing and deployment. Navigating multi-state operations requires understanding varying requirements.

Cybersecurity Standards:

UNECE WP.29 regulations mandate the implementation of automotive cybersecurity management systems. Vehicles must demonstrate cybersecurity by design and continuous monitoring.

SAE J3061 provides guidance on automotive cybersecurity processes. Threat modeling, risk assessment, and validation activities throughout the development lifecycle.

Implementation Guidance

Perception System Security:

Sensor Fusion combines multiple sensor modalities. Cameras, lidar, radar, and ultrasonic sensors provide complementary information. Cross-validation between sensors detects spoofing attempts.

Adversarial examples designed for cameras may not transfer to lidar. Sensor fusion reduces attack success probability. However, sophisticated attacks might target multiple modalities simultaneously.

Adversarial Robustness hardens vision systems against physical attacks. Train on adversarial examples, including physical perturbations. Test robustness against adversarial objects and lighting conditions.

Physical adversarial examples face constraints. Perturbations must survive real-world conditions, including viewing angles, lighting, and distance. This creates opportunities for detection.

Redundancy and Diversity provide fault tolerance. Multiple independent perception systems reduce single-point failures. Diverse architectures prevent common-mode failures from shared vulnerabilities.

Decision-Making Security:

Formal Verification proves safety properties for critical components. Model checking verifies that decision logic satisfies safety requirements. Verification provides mathematical guarantees stronger than testing.

However, verification scalability limits applicability. Complete systems resist full verification. Focus verification on safety-critical decision components.

Runtime Monitoring will detect anomalous behaviors. Compare planned actions against safety constraints. Unexpected behaviors trigger fallback to safe states. Conservative operation when uncertain prioritizes safety.

Fail-Safe Mechanisms ensure safe behavior during system failures. Loss of perception should trigger a safe stop maneuver. Communication failures should default to conservative behavior. Design for graceful degradation under attack.

Communication Security:

Authentication prevents message injection. Cryptographic signatures prove message authenticity. Recipients verify signatures before acting on messages.

Encryption protects message confidentiality. Sensitive information like location and routing should not be visible to eavesdroppers. However, latency requirements constrain cryptographic choices.

Intrusion Detection identifies compromised vehicles. Unusual messaging patterns indicate potential compromise. Collaborative intrusion detection shares threat intelligence across vehicle fleets.

Update Security:

Secure Boot ensures only authorized software executes. Cryptographic verification during boot prevents the execution of compromised firmware. Hardware root of trust provides a security foundation.

Over-the-Air Updates enable rapid vulnerability patching. Cryptographic signatures prevent malicious update injection. Staged rollouts detect problems before fleet-wide deployment.

However, updates create attack windows. Carefully manage update timing and validation. Enable rapid rollback if updates cause problems.

Case Study: Adversarial Stop Sign Attack

Researchers demonstrated that adversarial stickers on stop signs caused autonomous vehicles to misclassify them as speed limit signs. The attack worked across viewing angles and lighting conditions.

Implications: Physical adversarial attacks pose real-world risks to autonomous vehicles. Adversarial perturbations need not be subtle to be effective. Simple modifications accessible to vandals could cause safety hazards.

Industry Response: Automotive manufacturers enhanced adversarial training, including the introduction of physical perturbations. Sensor fusion provides defense through diversity. Monitoring detects unusual classification patterns.

Ongoing Challenges: Complete defense against physical adversarial objects remains elusive. Trade-offs between sensitivity and specificity complicate detection. Standardized testing protocols for adversarial robustness are still emerging.

Lessons: Academic security research reveals real vulnerabilities. Physical world deployment creates attack vectors beyond digital adversarial examples. Safety-critical systems require defense against creative physical attacks.

6.6 Cross-Industry Considerations

Supply Chain Security

All industries face AI supply chain risks. Pre-trained models from unknown sources might contain backdoors. Third-party libraries could have vulnerabilities. Cloud AI services might not provide adequate security.

Vendor Assessment evaluates AI suppliers' security practices. Require security documentation, third-party audits, and vulnerability disclosure programs. Contractual security requirements clarify expectations.

Model Provenance tracks models throughout their lifecycle. Document training data sources, development procedures, and validation results. Provenance enables assessing trustworthiness and liability.

Component Security Testing validates third-party AI components. Test for backdoors, adversarial vulnerabilities, and privacy leakage before deployment. Treat external models with appropriate skepticism.

Regulatory Compliance Management

Organizations operating across industries face complex compliance landscapes. Consistent practices spanning sectors reduce complexity.

The Compliance Framework establishes a systematic approach to regulatory requirements. Inventory applicable regulations and standards. Map requirements to controls and validation procedures.

Documentation Standards provide consistent compliance evidence. Standardized documentation templates reduce duplicated effort. Central repositories enable audits across business units.

Continuous Compliance monitors ongoing adherence. Automated compliance checking detects violations early. Regular audits validate that controls operate effectively.

Incident Response Coordination

Security incidents may span multiple business units and industries. Coordinated response proves essential.

Central Security Operations provides consistent monitoring and response. Security Operations Centers (SOCs) aggregate alerts from distributed systems. Standardized incident response procedures enable efficient handling.

Information Sharing enables learning from others' incidents. Industry-specific Information Sharing and Analysis Centers (ISACs) distribute threat intelligence. Participation improves organizational security while strengthening sector resilience.

Cross-Functional Teams address incidents comprehensively. Technical, legal, communications, and business stakeholders must coordinate. Clear roles and communication channels prevent confusion during high-stress response.

Chapter Summary

This chapter explored AI security implementation across the following major industries:

Healthcare: Privacy regulations, patient safety requirements, and extensive testing create unique challenges. Federated learning, adversarial robustness, and explainability address healthcare-specific concerns. Bias mitigation ensures equitable care across patient populations.

Financial Services: Adversarial environments, real-time requirements, and regulatory requirements for fairness shape financial AI security. Ensemble fraud detection, explainable credit scoring, and trading algorithm controls address sector-specific threats.

Manufacturing: Physical safety, operational continuity, and supply chain complexity characterize manufacturing AI. Sensor validation, adversarial robustness for quality control, and secure industrial IoT practices protect manufacturing systems.

Retail: Customer experience, privacy concerns, and bot attacks define the challenges of retail AI. Robust recommendations, dynamic pricing, security, and privacy-preserving analytics balance functionality with protection.

Transportation: Safety criticality, real-time constraints, and physical attacks characterize autonomous systems. Sensor fusion, formal verification, and secure communication address transportation-specific risks.

Cross-Industry: Supply chain security, compliance management, and incident response coordination apply across sectors. Consistent practices reduce complexity while addressing shared challenges.

Industry context fundamentally shapes the implementation of AI security. Threat models, regulatory requirements, and operational constraints vary across sectors. Effective security requires understanding industry-specific characteristics and adapting general principles accordingly.

Key Takeaways

1. Industry context determines appropriate security measures. Healthcare's privacy focus differs from manufacturing's safety emphasis. Generic approaches prove insufficient for sector-specific challenges.

2. Regulatory requirements vary dramatically across industries. Understanding applicable regulations guides security implementations. Proactive compliance proves more effective than reactive remediation.

3. Threat models must reflect industry-specific adversaries and motivations. Financial systems face organized criminals, while healthcare faces privacy violations. Different adversaries require different defenses.

4. Operational constraints shape feasible security measures. Real-time trading requires low-latency defenses. Manufacturing equipment lifetimes complicate patching. Understanding constraints enables practical solutions.

5. Cross-industry concerns like supply chain security affect all sectors. Consistent approaches to shared challenges reduce complexity while maintaining effectiveness.

6. Case studies reveal real-world consequences of security failures. Learning from others' incidents improves organizational security without repeating mistakes.

7. Industry-specific standards and best practices provide proven frameworks. Leveraging existing standards accelerates security maturity while ensuring completeness.

Reflection Questions

1. Compare healthcare AI privacy requirements with retail customer data practices. How do different regulatory frameworks reflect different societal values about data protection?

2. If you must prioritize between adversarial robustness and fairness for a credit scoring model, how would you make this decision? What factors would inform your priority?

3. Consider autonomous vehicle perception systems. How would you design testing procedures that validate security against physical adversarial attacks while ensuring testing doesn't create public safety risks?

4. How do real-time processing requirements in financial trading systems constrain defensive options? What security measures remain feasible under strict latency requirements?

5. Manufacturing equipment often operates for decades. How do you secure AI systems deployed on equipment that may outlive current security assumptions and practices?

6. Compare incident response for healthcare data breaches versus financial system compromises. How do different notification requirements and stakeholder concerns shape response strategies?

7. What tensions exist between competitive advantage from proprietary AI systems and information sharing, improving industry-wide security? How should organizations balance these competing interests?

7

Advanced Technologies and Future Directions

Learning Objectives

By the end of this chapter, you will:

- Understand quantum computing's implications for AI security
- Implement privacy-preserving machine learning techniques, including federated learning and secure multi-party computation
- Apply advanced cryptographic methods to AI systems
- Deploy explainability techniques that enhance security and accountability
- Leverage AI for cybersecurity defense and threat detection
- Anticipate emerging threats from foundation models and autonomous systems
- Design security architectures resilient to future attack vectors
- Evaluate cutting-edge defensive technologies for practical deployment

Introduction: The Evolving Frontier

AI security remains a rapidly evolving field. Techniques considered state-of-the-art today may become obsolete tomorrow. New attack vectors emerge as AI capabilities advance. Defensive technologies mature from research concepts to practical deployments. Understanding emerging trends and future directions enables proactive preparation rather than reactive scrambling.

This chapter explores advanced technologies shaping the future of AI security. We examine cryptographic innovations enabling privacy-preserving computation. We investigate the implications of quantum computing for both threats and defenses. We explore how AI itself can become a security tool that defends against attacks. We analyze emerging risks from increasingly powerful AI systems.

The technologies presented here vary in maturity. Some have transitioned to production deployment. Others remain research prototypes requiring further development. Some represent incremental improvements to existing techniques. Others promise paradigm shifts in how we approach AI security. Understanding this spectrum enables strategic planning for the evolution of security.

We emphasize practical considerations throughout. For each technology, we assess current capabilities, deployment readiness, computational costs, and limitations. This grounded perspective helps distinguish hype from genuine advancement. It enables informed decisions about which technologies warrant investment today versus which require continued monitoring.

7.1 Quantum Computing and AI Security

Quantum Threat Landscape

Quantum computing poses existential threats to current cryptographic systems. Shor's algorithm enables quantum computers to factor large integers and efficiently compute discrete logarithms. This breaks RSA, Diffie-Hellman, and elliptic curve cryptography that protect most current systems. Grover's algorithm provides quadratic speedups for unstructured search, weakening symmetric encryption and hash functions.

Timeline Considerations affect the urgency of quantum preparations. Current quantum computers remain small and error-prone. Reaching scales threatening cryptographic systems requires significant advances. Estimates vary widely, from ten to thirty years or more. However, "harvest now, decrypt later" attacks create urgency. Adversaries capture encrypted data today, storing it for decryption once quantum computers become available.

This threat model particularly concerns long-lived secrets. Medical records, government documents, and intellectual property may remain sensitive for decades. Data encrypted today with quantum-vulnerable algorithms will be exposed when quantum computers mature. Migration to quantum-resistant cryptography becomes urgent for protecting long-term secrets.

AI-Specific Implications extend beyond general cryptographic threats. Quantum algorithms might accelerate the generation of adversarial examples. Quantum optimization could improve the effectiveness of data poisoning attacks. Quantum machine learning algorithms might learn patterns that classical systems miss. Understanding these AI-specific quantum threats remains an active research area.

Post-Quantum Cryptography

Post-quantum cryptography provides cryptographic algorithms resistant to quantum attacks. These algorithms rely on mathematical problems believed to be hard for both classical and quantum computers. NIST's post-quantum cryptography standardization process selected algorithms for different use cases.

Lattice-Based Cryptography relies on the hardness of lattice problems. CRYSTALS-Kyber provides key encapsulation with strong security guarantees. Lattice-based schemes offer good performance and reasonable key sizes. Security reductions to well-studied hard problems provide confidence in long-term security.

Implementation requires careful attention to side-channel attacks. Many lattice operations leak timing or power information. Constant-time implementations resist timing attacks. Masking techniques protect against power analysis. These countermeasures add complexity but prove essential for secure deployment.

Hash-Based Signatures provide post-quantum digital signatures. SPHINCS+ achieves stateless signatures with conservative security assumptions. These schemes rely only on hash function security, providing strong confidence. However, signature sizes are substantial, potentially limiting some applications.

Stateless operation simplifies deployment compared to earlier stateful hash-based signatures. No state synchronization requirements reduce implementation complexity. The trade-off is larger signatures compared to stateful alternatives.

Code-Based Cryptography uses error-correcting codes. Classic McEliece provides public-key encryption with a long security history. Decades of cryptanalysis provide confidence in underlying hardness assumptions. However, public keys are very large, limiting deployment in resource-constrained environments.

Structured variants reduce key sizes but face less cryptanalytic scrutiny. Trade-offs between efficiency and conservative security require careful evaluation for specific deployments.

Implementation Strategies for migrating to post-quantum cryptography:

Hybrid Approaches combine classical and post-quantum algorithms. Communications encrypted with both RSA and Kyber remain secure if either algorithm is unbroken. This defense-in-depth strategy provides security during the transition period. The performance overhead is modest compared to the security benefits.

Crypto-Agility enables algorithm transitions without a complete system redesign. Modular cryptographic libraries abstract algorithm choices. Protocol negotiation enables gradual migration. This flexibility is essential given the ongoing evolution of post-quantum cryptography.

Migration Planning requires systematic approaches. Inventory all cryptographic uses across systems. Prioritize high-value, long-lived secrets for early migration. Test post-quantum implementations thoroughly before production deployment. Staged rollouts minimize disruption while ensuring security.

Quantum Machine Learning Security

Quantum machine learning explores the application of quantum algorithms to machine learning tasks. While large-scale quantum machine learning remains distant, understanding security implications proves important for long-term planning.

Quantum Advantage in Attacks might accelerate the generation of adversarial examples. Quantum algorithms for optimization could find smaller perturbations more efficiently. Quantum amplitude estimation might improve the effectiveness of membership inference attacks. These potential advantages remain mostly theoretical until practical quantum computers are available.

Quantum-Enhanced Defenses might improve security. Quantum random number generation provides true randomness for cryptographic applications. Quantum key distribution enables provably secure key exchange. These quantum technologies are available today, though with limited deployment.

Quantum Neural Networks represent entirely new computational paradigms. Security properties of quantum machine learning models remain poorly understood. As quantum machine learning matures, security research must keep pace. Early consideration of security prevents embedding vulnerabilities in new paradigms.

7.2 Privacy-Preserving Machine Learning

Federated Learning

Federated learning enables training models on distributed data without centralization. Participants train on local data and share only model updates. Central servers aggregate updates to produce global models. This approach addresses privacy by keeping sensitive data local.

Architecture Variants suit different scenarios:

Cross-Device Federated Learning involves many devices, such as smartphones. Devices join training rounds as they become available. High device counts provide natural privacy through aggregation. Communication efficiency becomes critical with constrained networks. Compression and quantization reduce communication overhead.

Cross-Silo Federated Learning involves organizations like hospitals or banks. Fewer participants with reliable connections enable different protocols. Higher trust assumptions permit more complex coordination. Privacy protection focuses on the isolation of inter-organizational data.

Security Challenges in federated learning:

Byzantine Attacks involve malicious participants submitting corrupted updates. Malicious updates can poison global models or compromise privacy. Defense requires robust aggregation, detection, and exclusion of outlier updates. However, distinguishing malicious updates from unusual but legitimate updates proves difficult.

Reputation systems track participant reliability. New participants face greater scrutiny. Consistently high-quality participants earn trust. However, patient adversaries might build a reputation before attacking.

Privacy Attacks threaten despite data localization. Model updates leak information about local training data. Gradient analysis can reveal training examples. Multiple update observations improve reconstruction attacks. Privacy protections must extend beyond data centralization.

Secure Aggregation prevents coordinators from seeing individual updates. Cryptographic protocols ensure servers learn only aggregated values. Participants cannot be identified from their specific contributions. This provides formal privacy guarantees against honest-but-curious servers.

However, secure aggregation adds computational and communication overhead. Coordination complexity increases with participant count. Dropout handling requires careful protocol design. These costs must be weighed against privacy benefits.

Differential Privacy in Federated Learning provides mathematical privacy guarantees. Adding calibrated noise to gradients before sharing ensures privacy. Composition theorems bound total privacy loss across training. This approach provides strong theoretical guarantees.

The challenge is balancing privacy and utility. Strong privacy budgets add substantial noise, reducing model accuracy. Weak privacy budgets provide limited protection. Finding acceptable trade-offs requires understanding privacy requirements and utility needs.

Practical Deployments demonstrate federated learning viability:

Smartphone keyboard prediction trains on-device without uploading personal text. Healthcare consortia enable collaborative research without sharing patient records. Financial institutions detect fraud patterns while protecting transaction privacy. These deployments validate the practical utility of federated learning.

Secure Multi-Party Computation

Secure multi-party computation (SMPC) enables joint computation on private inputs. Multiple parties compute functions of their combined data without revealing individual inputs. Cryptographic protocols ensure no party learns others' private information beyond what the function outputs reveal.

SMPC Protocols:

Secret Sharing splits a secret into shares distributed among parties. No individual share reveals information about the secret. Reconstructing the secret requires combining sufficient shares. Linear secret sharing enables efficient computation on shared values.

Shamir's secret sharing provides threshold properties. Any t of n shares can reconstruct the secret. Fewer than t shares reveal no information. This flexibility suits various trust assumptions. However, communication requirements increase with the number of participants.

Garbled Circuits enable secure two-party computation. One party creates an encrypted circuit representation. The other party evaluates the garbled circuit on encrypted inputs. Only the final output decrypts, hiding intermediate computations. Yao's protocol pioneered this approach.

Modern improvements dramatically reduce costs. Free XOR optimization eliminates the cost of XOR gates. Half-gates reduce AND gate costs. These optimizations make garbled circuits practical for moderately sized computations.

Homomorphic Secret Sharing enables efficient multiparty computation. Parties hold shares enabling local computation. Periodic communication synchronizes shares. This approach proves more efficient than generic SMPC for many computations. However, it supports only a limited set of function families.

SMPC for Machine Learning:

Secure Training enables collaborative model training without data sharing. Parties provide encrypted training data. SMPC protocols compute model updates. The final model parameters are revealed, but the training data remains private. This approach enables use cases impossible with data centralization.

Healthcare research exemplifies secure training value. Hospitals provide patient data for model training. Individual patient records never leave hospitals. Research benefits from large, combined datasets without violating privacy.

Secure Inference enables prediction on encrypted data. Users submit encrypted queries. Servers compute predictions on encrypted data. Only users can decrypt results. This protects both model intellectual property and user privacy.

However, performance remains challenging. SMPC adds significant computational overhead. Secure training takes orders of magnitude longer than plaintext training. Secure inference latency often proves unacceptable for real-time applications. Ongoing research improves efficiency, but practical limitations remain.

Homomorphic Encryption

Homomorphic encryption enables computation on encrypted data. Operations on ciphertexts produce encrypted results. Decryption reveals the same result as performing operations on plaintexts. This provides ultimate privacy: data never decrypts during processing.

Homomorphic Encryption Types:

Partially Homomorphic Encryption supports limited operations. Paillier encryption enables addition on encrypted values. RSA supports multiplication. ElGamal provides other algebraic properties. Partial homomorphisms suffice for specific applications but limit general computation.

Somewhat Homomorphic Encryption supports only a limited depth of operations. Each operation adds noise to ciphertexts. After a sufficient number of operations, noise overwhelms the signal. Computation depth is bounded by the accumulation of noise. This enables simple computations but not complex algorithms.

Fully Homomorphic Encryption (FHE) supports arbitrary computations. Bootstrapping procedures refresh noisy ciphertexts. This enables unlimited computation depth. However, bootstrapping is extremely expensive. Practical FHE requires careful algorithm design that minimizes bootstrapping.

FHE Schemes:

BGV and BFV schemes support exact integer arithmetic. SIMD operations process multiple values simultaneously. These schemes suit applications requiring exact computation. Parameter selection trades security level against performance.

CKKS enables approximate arithmetic on real numbers. Native support for floating-point-like operations. This scheme suits machine learning tasks that require approximate computation. However, the approximate nature affects some applications.

TFHE optimizes for Boolean circuits. Fast bootstrapping enables practical encrypted computation. This scheme particularly suits applications naturally expressed as Boolean operations. Neural network inference can be compiled to Boolean circuits.

Machine Learning with FHE:

Encrypted Inference protects both model and query privacy. Users encrypt inputs before sending to servers. Servers compute predictions on encrypted data. Only users can decrypt predictions. Neither server learns queries nor users learn model parameters.

However, inference latency is substantial. Even optimized implementations take seconds for simple models. Neural network inference requires millions of operations. Each homomorphic operation is expensive. Current FHE suits low-frequency high-value queries, not real-time services.

Encrypted Training remains largely impractical. Training requires many more operations than inference. Gradient computation and parameter updates multiply computational costs. Current FHE cannot support practical neural network training. Research continues to pursue efficient training, but practical solutions remain distant.

Practical Considerations:

FHE performance improves steadily but remains orders of magnitude slower than plaintext computation. Careful algorithm design minimizes expensive operations. Hybrid approaches combine FHE with other techniques. Preprocessing in plaintext before encryption reduces the computational cost of encryption.

Parameter selection involves security-performance trade-offs. Larger parameters provide stronger security but degrade performance. Understanding threat models guides appropriate parameter choices. Conservative parameters suit long-term secrets while aggressive parameters enable better performance for shorter-lived data.

7.3 Explainability for Security

Explainability Techniques

Explainability enables understanding model decisions. Security applications include debugging, auditing, and detecting attacks. Different techniques provide different insights suited to various security needs.

Feature Attribution Methods identify important input features:

LIME (Local Interpretable Model-agnostic Explanations) approximates complex models locally using simpler ones. For any prediction, LIME identifies which features most influenced the decision. The technique works with any model by treating it as a black box. However, local approximations may not reflect global model behavior.

SHAP (SHapley Additive exPlanations) provides game-theoretic feature importance. Based on Shapley values from cooperative game theory, SHAP satisfies desirable theoretical properties. Consistent attribution helps in understanding model behavior. However, computing exact SHAP values is expensive for complex models.

Integrated Gradients compute feature importance through path integration. Starting from baseline input, integrate gradients along the path to the actual input. This attribution method satisfies nice theoretical properties. Path choice affects attributions, underscoring the need for careful baseline selection.

Example-Based Methods explain through similar examples:

Influence Functions identify training examples that most affect predictions. Computing influence requires Hessian information, which is expensive for large models. However, influence functions directly connect predictions to training data. This proves valuable for detecting data poisoning.

Prototypes and Criticisms find representative and unusual training examples. Prototypes characterize typical examples for each class. Criticisms identify unusual examples not well-represented by prototypes. This provides an intuitive explanation through concrete examples.

Concept-Based Methods explain through high-level concepts:

TCAV (Testing with Concept Activation Vectors) measures concept importance. Define concepts through example sets. Measure prediction sensitivity to concepts. This enables explanations using human-understandable concepts rather than low-level features.

Concept definition requires domain expertise. Choosing meaningful concepts proves challenging. However, concept-based explanations provide an intuitive understanding bridging human and model representations.

Security Applications

Detecting Data Poisoning through explanation analysis:

Poisoned models exhibit unusual feature dependencies. Backdoor triggers create strong feature importance for trigger patterns. Comparing explanations across inputs reveals anomalous patterns. Systematic explanation analysis detects potential poisoning.

However, sophisticated attacks craft stealthy backdoors. Explanations may not reveal subtle poisoning. Combining explanation analysis with other detection methods improves reliability.

Verifying Model Behavior through explanation validation:

Explanations should align with domain knowledge. A medical diagnosis model attributing importance to irrelevant features indicates problems. Systematic explanation review catches spurious correlations and potential biases.

However, explanations are not necessarily faithful to model computation. Post-hoc explanations may misrepresent the model's actual logic. Validating explanation faithfulness requires careful methodology.

Debugging Adversarial Examples through perturbation analysis:

Explanations reveal how adversarial perturbations affect predictions. Comparing explanations for clean and adversarial examples identifies vulnerability sources. This understanding informs defense development.

Attribution methods identify which perturbations most impact predictions. Focusing defenses on critical features improves efficiency. However, adaptive attacks might exploit explanation-guided defenses.

Supporting Auditing and Compliance:

Explainability enables demonstrating regulatory compliance. Fair lending laws require that credit decisions be explained. GDPR creates expectations for automated decisions. Systematic explanation generation supports compliance documentation.

However, legal explanation requirements remain ambiguous. Technical explanations may not satisfy legal standards. Close coordination between technical and legal teams proves essential.

Limitations and Challenges

Explanation: Faithfulness concerns whether explanations accurately reflect model behavior. Many explanation techniques provide plausible post-hoc rationalizations rather than true mechanistic understanding. Adversaries might exploit this gap, creating models that behave correctly on tests but incorrectly in practice.

Validating faithfulness requires careful evaluation. Compare explanations to ground truth when available. Test consistency across similar inputs. However, complete faithfulness verification remains difficult.

Computational Costs limit explanation deployment. Some techniques require multiple model evaluations per explanation. Real-time systems may not tolerate the overhead of explanation. Trade-offs between explanation quality and computational efficiency require careful navigation.

Adversarial Manipulation of explanations represents an emerging threat. Attackers craft models providing misleading explanations, concealing malicious behavior. Robust explanations resistant to manipulation remain an open research problem.

7.4 AI-Driven Cybersecurity

AI for Threat Detection

AI enhances cybersecurity by processing vast amounts of data and identifying threats that humans might miss. Machine learning detects anomalies, classifies malware, and predicts attacks. However, AI security tools themselves become targets of attack.

Anomaly Detection Systems:

Unsupervised Learning identifies unusual patterns without labeled attacks. Autoencoders learn normal behavior by reconstructing inputs. High reconstruction error indicates anomalies. Clustering algorithms group similar behaviors, with outliers indicating potential threats.

However, legitimate behavior varies widely. Normal variation creates false positives. Adversaries gradually shifting behavior might evade detection through concept drift. Balancing sensitivity and specificity remains challenging.

Supervised Learning classifies known threat patterns. Training on labeled attacks and benign activities. Neural networks, random forests, and gradient boosting machines achieve high accuracy. Regular retraining maintains effectiveness against evolving threats.

However, novel attacks evade signature-based detection. Adversaries study detection systems and craft evasion techniques. Supervised learning complements but cannot replace human expertise.

Behavioral Analysis:

User and Entity Behavior Analytics (UEBA) profiles normal user and system behavior. Deviations from established baselines trigger alerts. Machine learning adapts baselines as behaviors legitimately evolve. This approach catches insider threats and compromised accounts.

However, user behavior varies naturally. Travel, role changes, and unusual but legitimate activities create false positives. Careful baseline establishment and threshold tuning prove critical.

Network Traffic Analysis identifies anomalous communication patterns. Protocol analysis, timing patterns, and volume analysis detect malicious activities. Deep packet inspection combined with machine learning can improve detection.

Encrypted traffic limits analysis opportunities. Privacy protections restrict deep inspection. Metadata analysis provides partial visibility but misses attack details.

Automated Incident Response

AI-Powered Orchestration automates response workflows. Security Orchestration, Automation, and Response (SOAR) platforms integrate disparate security tools. Machine learning prioritizes alerts, reducing analyst workload. Automated playbooks execute common response actions.

However, automation risks propagating errors. Incorrect automated responses might worsen incidents. Human oversight remains essential for high-stakes decisions.

Intelligent Alert Triage reduces the burden of false positives. Machine learning classifies alerts by severity and likelihood. Historical incident data trains triage models. This helps analysts focus on genuine threats.

Context aggregation from multiple sources improves triage accuracy. Combining network, endpoint, and identity signals provides a holistic view. However, sophisticated attacks craft contexts that appear benign.

Predictive Threat Intelligence:

Attack Forecasting predicts likely future attacks. Analyzing historical attack patterns, geopolitical events, and vulnerability disclosures. Machine learning identifies leading indicators of attacks. This enables proactive defense deployment.

However, prediction accuracy remains limited. Novel attack vectors lack historical patterns. Adversaries adapt strategies to defeat prediction. Forecasts should inform, not replace, defense-in-depth.

Adversarial Machine Learning for Security

Applying adversarial machine learning principles to cybersecurity creates robust defenses. Understanding how attackers might evade detection informs defensive improvements.

Adversarial Training for Malware Detection:

Training on adversarial malware samples improves detection robustness. Generate evasion attempts through automated perturbation. Include adversarial examples in training. This hardens classifiers against evasion.

However, generating adversarial malware is difficult. Maintaining malicious functionality while evading detection constrains the scope of perturbations. Generative adversarial networks show promise but face challenges in the malware domain.

Red Team AI:

Automated red teams generate novel attacks testing defenses. Reinforcement learning agents learn to evade detection. This provides continuous security testing. Discovering vulnerabilities before real attackers enables proactive patching.

However, automated red teams lack human creativity. Human red teamers combine tools with lateral thinking. Hybrid human-AI red teams prove most effective.

Security of AI Security Tools

AI security tools themselves are subject to adversarial attacks. Adversaries poison security training data or craft evasion techniques. Securing AI security tools requires special attention.

Training Data Integrity proves critical for security ML. Malicious training data creates blind spots or backdoors. Carefully validate security training data provenance. Monitor for distribution shifts indicating poisoning.

Evasion Resistance requires adversarial robustness. Attackers specifically target security ML systems. Adversarial training and robust architectures improve resilience. Regular testing against evasion techniques validates effectiveness.

Model Extraction Prevention protects security ML intellectual property. Adversaries systematically query systems learning their behavior. Rate limiting, noise injection, and query monitoring defend against extraction. However, extraction resistance must not compromise detection capabilities.

7.5 Emerging Threats

Foundation Model Risks

Large language models and other foundation models create new security challenges. Their scale, capabilities, and wide deployment amplify traditional threats while introducing novel risks.

Dual-Use Concerns:

Foundation models enable beneficial applications but also malicious uses. Code generation assists developers, but also creates malware. Text generation produces both helpful content and disinformation. Image generation creates art but also deepfakes.

Preventing dual use proves extremely difficult. Use restrictions are easily bypassed. Open-source models face no restrictions. Focusing on detection and mitigation rather than prevention proves more practical.

Jailbreaking and Prompt Injection:

Safety measures in foundation models are continually bypassed. Jailbreaking discovers prompts to circumvent restrictions. Prompt injection embeds malicious instructions in inputs. These attacks exploit fundamental properties of language models.

Arms races between developers adding restrictions and users finding bypasses continue escalating. Perfect prevention appears impossible. Defense requires layered approaches, including input filtering, output filtering, and monitoring.

Training Data Extraction:

Large language models memorize training data, including sensitive information. Adversaries extract names, phone numbers, email addresses, and confidential documents. Scale amplifies memorization risks. Billions of training examples increase the probability of memorizing sensitive information.

Differential privacy during training provides partial mitigation. However, privacy-utility trade-offs become severe at a large scale. Perfect privacy is impossible while maintaining utility. Risk management focuses on minimizing the exposure of sensitive data during training.

Model Repurposing:

Openly available foundation models can be fine-tuned for malicious purposes. Small fine-tuning datasets adapt models to harmful tasks. This democratizes harmful AI capabilities. Monitoring for malicious fine-tuning proves challenging.

Release strategies balance openness and security. Staged releases with monitoring enable misuse detection. Restricted access to the most powerful models limits some risks. However, model proliferation makes control increasingly difficult.

Autonomous System Risks

Increasingly autonomous AI systems create safety and security challenges. Reduced human oversight increases the consequences of failures. Autonomy enables new attack vectors.

Goal Misalignment:

AI systems optimize stated objectives, which may diverge from intended goals. Specification gaming finds unintended ways to maximize metrics. Goodhart's Law states that "when a measure becomes a target, it ceases to be a good measure." This affects autonomous systems pursuing misspecified objectives.

Robust objective specification remains difficult. Alignment research develops techniques to ensure that AI systems pursue their intended goals. However, perfect alignment may be fundamentally impossible. Defense requires monitoring and intervention capabilities.

Emergent Behaviors:

Complex AI systems exhibit behaviors not explicitly programmed. Interactions between components create emergent properties. Some emergent behaviors prove beneficial. Others create safety or security issues.

Comprehensive testing cannot cover all possible emergent behaviors. Formal verification faces scalability challenges. Runtime monitoring and intervention capabilities provide a fallback when unexpected behaviors emerge.

Cascading Failures:

Interconnected AI systems create risks of failure propagation. Errors in one system trigger failures in dependent systems. Feedback loops amplify small problems into large catastrophes. Financial flash crashes demonstrate these risks.

Defense requires circuit breakers that interrupt cascade propagation. Isolation limits failure spread. Diversity prevents common mode failures. However, completely preventing cascades in complex systems proves impossible.

Synthetic Media Threats

Generative AI creates increasingly realistic synthetic media. Deepfakes, voice cloning, and image generation enable sophisticated deception. Security implications span authentication, information integrity, and social manipulation.

Authentication Challenges:

Biometric authentication faces deepfake threats. Synthetic faces, voices, and videos can impersonate individuals. Liveness detection becomes critical but is vulnerable to adversarial attacks. Deepfake technology advances faster than detection.

Multi-factor authentication, combining biometrics with other factors, provides defense. However, increasingly realistic synthesis threatens multiple modalities. Authentication systems must evolve continuously.

Disinformation at Scale:

Generative AI enables the production of disinformation at an unprecedented scale. Automated content creation floods information environments. Detection struggles to keep pace with the generation. Human fact-checking cannot scale to keep pace with generation rates.

Provenance tracking helps identify synthetic content. Cryptographic signatures prove content authenticity. However, adversaries create content without signatures. Detection must complement provenance.

Social Engineering Enhancement:

AI-generated content makes phishing and social engineering more effective. Personalized messages using language models increase success rates. Voice cloning enables phone-based attacks. These capabilities lower attack barriers.

Security awareness training must address AI-enhanced attacks. Technical defenses, such as sender verification, provide only partial protection. However, human judgment remains vulnerable to sophisticated AI-generated deception.

7.6 Future-Proofing AI Security

Anticipatory Security

Future-proofing requires anticipating tomorrow's threats today. Long development cycles mean that security designed today faces threats that emerge years later. Defensive architectures must accommodate unknown future capabilities.

Threat Horizon Scanning:

Systematic monitoring of AI research reveals future capabilities. Academic papers preview techniques that become practical years later. Early awareness enables proactive defense development. However, distinguishing hype from genuine advancement proves difficult.

Participation in research communities provides an early warning. Attending conferences and reading preprints reveals emerging trends. However, this requires dedicated resources and expertise.

Capability-Based Threat Modeling:

Rather than modeling specific attacks, consider fundamental capabilities. What could adversaries achieve with infinite compute? With quantum computers? With AGI? Understanding capability limits informs long-term planning.

However, capability-based models may seem abstract. Translating abstract capabilities to concrete risks requires careful analysis. Combining capability-based and threat-based approaches provides comprehensive coverage.

Adaptive Security Architectures:

Design systems that evolve with threats. Modular architectures enable updating defenses without system redesign. API-based integration allows for the incorporation of new security technologies. Crypto-agility enables algorithm transitions.

However, adaptability introduces complexity. Overly flexible architectures may sacrifice performance. Balancing adaptability and efficiency requires careful design.

Research Directions

Several research directions promise significant improvements in security. Investment in these areas may yield breakthrough defenses.

Verified AI:

Formal verification provides mathematical guarantees about AI behavior. Model checking verifies properties against specifications. Theorem proving establishes correctness. While current techniques face scalability limits, steady progress continues.

Practical verified AI remains distant but achievable. Hybrid approaches verify critical components while empirically testing complete systems. This balanced approach makes verification tractable.

Interpretable-By-Design Models:

Rather than post-hoc explanation of black boxes, design inherently interpretable models. Attention mechanisms, prototype-based learning, and structured models provide transparency. Performance gaps between interpretable and black-box models narrow.

However, interpretability-performance trade-offs remain. Extremely complex tasks may require opaque models. The goal is interpretability sufficient for security rather than complete transparency.

Robust-By-Construction Learning:

Rather than hardening models post-training, build robustness into learning itself. Certified training provides robustness guarantees. Robust optimization directly optimizes worst-case rather than average-case performance. These techniques reduce the accuracy costs of robustness.

However, computational costs remain significant. Robust training takes longer than standard training. Performance improvements may eventually make robust training the default rather than a special effort.

Collaborative Security:

Collective defense aggregates information across organizations. Shared threat intelligence improves detection. Federated learning enables collaborative model training. Privacy-preserving techniques enable cooperation without exposing sensitive information.

However, collaboration requires trust and coordination. Competitive organizations hesitate to share information. Standard protocols and neutral intermediaries facilitate cooperation.

Ethical Considerations

Future security technologies raise ethical questions requiring careful consideration. Technical capabilities must align with societal values.

Surveillance Risks:

Advanced monitoring capabilities enable unprecedented surveillance. AI analyzes behavior, predicts actions, and detects anomalies. While these capabilities enhance security, they also threaten privacy and freedom.

Balancing security and civil liberties requires ongoing dialogue. Technical mechanisms like differential privacy provide some protection. However, governance and oversight prove equally important.

Autonomous Decision-Making:

Increasingly autonomous AI makes consequential decisions with limited human oversight. This efficiency enables new capabilities but raises accountability questions. Who is responsible when autonomous systems cause harm?

Maintaining meaningful human control remains essential. Clear accountability frameworks must establish responsibility. Technical measures like interpretability enable oversight.

Algorithmic Fairness:

Security measures must not systematically disadvantage protected groups. Facial recognition for security disproportionately misidentifies minorities. Fraud detection might unfairly target certain demographics. Security and fairness must be pursued jointly.

Regular fairness audits assess disparate impacts. Bias mitigation techniques reduce unfairness. However, perfect fairness remains elusive. Ongoing monitoring and adjustment prove necessary.

Chapter Summary

This chapter explored advanced technologies and future directions in AI security:

Quantum Computing: Post-quantum cryptography prepares for quantum threats. Migration strategies enable transitions before quantum computers mature. Quantum machine learning creates both opportunities and risks, requiring ongoing research.

Privacy-Preserving ML: Federated learning enables collaborative training without centralizing data. Secure multi-party computation and homomorphic encryption provide cryptographic privacy. These technologies enable beneficial AI while protecting sensitive information.

Explainability: Feature attribution, example-based, and concept-based explanations support security. Applications include detecting poisoning, verifying behavior, and supporting compliance. However, explaining faithfulness and computational costs remains a challenge.

AI-Driven Cybersecurity: AI improves threat detection, automates response, and provides predictive intelligence. However, AI security tools themselves become targets of attack. Securing security AI requires special attention.

Emerging Threats: Foundation models, autonomous systems, and synthetic media create novel risks. Dual-use concerns, goal misalignment, and disinformation at scale challenge security. Proactive approaches prepare for these evolving threats.

Future-Proofing: Anticipatory security, capability-based threat modeling, and adaptive architectures prepare for unknown future threats. Research in verified AI, interpretable models, and robust learning promises fundamental improvements. Ethical considerations ensure technical capabilities align with societal values.

The AI security landscape continues evolving rapidly. Technologies considered cutting-edge today may become standard practice tomorrow. Staying informed about emerging technologies and threats enables proactive security rather than reactive crisis management.

Key Takeaways

1. Quantum computing threatens current cryptography, requiring migration to post-quantum algorithms. "Harvest now, decrypt later" attacks create urgency for protecting long-term secrets.

2. Privacy-preserving machine learning enables beneficial applications while protecting sensitive data. Federated learning, SMPC, and homomorphic encryption each suit different use cases with different trade-offs.

3. Explainability enhances security through debugging, auditing, and attack detection. However, explanation faithfulness and computational costs require careful consideration.

4. AI improves cybersecurity, but AI security tools themselves face adversarial attacks. Securing security AI requires robustness, integrity protection, and extraction resistance.

5. Foundation models, autonomous systems, and synthetic media create emerging threats. Dual-use concerns, jailbreaking, and disinformation at scale require new defensive approaches.

6. Future-proofing requires anticipating tomorrow's threats today. Adaptive architectures, capability-based threat modeling, and research investment prepare for evolution.

7. Ethical considerations ensure security technologies align with societal values. Surveillance risks, autonomous decision-making, and algorithmic fairness require ongoing attention.

Reflection Questions

1. Consider an organization storing encrypted medical records today. How urgently should they migrate to post-quantum cryptography? What factors influence this decision?

2. Compare federated learning, secure multi-party computation, and homomorphic encryption for a multi-hospital medical research scenario. Which approach best balances privacy, utility, and practicality?

3. If explanation techniques reveal adversarial vulnerabilities in your model, how do you balance publishing explanations for accountability versus withholding them for security?

4. As AI security tools become more powerful, how do you prevent adversaries from using those same tools to develop more sophisticated attacks?

5. Foundation models enable both beneficial and harmful applications. What strategies balance openness that enables innovation with restrictions that prevent misuse?

6. How would you design an adaptive security architecture that remains effective as AI capabilities advance beyond current anticipation?

7. What governance mechanisms ensure that security technologies advancing surveillance capabilities respect civil liberties and privacy?

8

The Future of AI Security

Learning Objectives

By the end of this chapter, you will:

- Understand how AI security is evolving as an organizational discipline
- Assess your organization's AI security maturity and identify improvement paths
- Navigate the developing standards and regulatory ecosystem
- Build effective AI security programs that scale with organizational needs
- Foster cross-functional collaboration essential for comprehensive security
- Anticipate long-term trends shaping AI security over the next decade

- Contribute to the broader AI security community through knowledge sharing
- Prepare strategically for an AI-driven future

Introduction: Beyond Technical Solutions

The previous chapters equipped you with technical knowledge about AI threats, defenses, and emerging technologies. This final chapter shifts perspective from technical implementation to organizational strategy and ecosystem evolution. AI security increasingly transcends purely technical challenges to become an organizational capability requiring strategic thinking, cross-functional collaboration, and sustained investment.

We stand at a critical juncture. Early adopters have learned hard lessons about AI security through incident response and remediation. Standards bodies are codifying best practices into formal frameworks. Regulators are moving from guidance to enforcement. The field is maturing from ad hoc experimentation to systematic practice.

This chapter examines the future of AI security across three dimensions. First, we explore organizational maturity models that guide systematic capability building. Second, we analyze the evolving ecosystem of standards, regulations, and shared infrastructure. Third, we project long-term trends that will shape the field over the coming decade.

Understanding these strategic dimensions enables you to position your organization for success as AI security matures from emerging practice to established discipline.

8.1 Organizational Maturity in AI Security

The Maturity Imperative

Most organizations find themselves somewhere between reactive firefighting and proactive security. Maturity models provide roadmaps for systematic improvement. They define capability levels, identify gaps, and suggest progression paths. Understanding where your organization stands enables realistic planning and resource allocation.

AI security maturity encompasses multiple dimensions. Technical capabilities represent only one aspect. Organizational structure, governance processes, cultural attitudes, talent development, and stakeholder engagement all contribute. Mature organizations excel across all dimensions rather than optimizing any single factor.

Maturity Level Framework

Level 1: Initial and Reactive

Organizations at this level address AI security issues as they arise, without a systematic approach. Security activities happen sporadically in response to incidents or external pressure. Documentation is minimal or nonexistent. Responsibilities remain unclear. Success depends on individual heroics rather than repeatable processes.

Characteristics include ad hoc security reviews conducted only when required, reactive incident response with no preparation, limited awareness of AI-specific threats, no dedicated AI security resources, and the absence of formal policies or procedures. Many organizations begin here, particularly those new to AI deployment or to security more generally.

The primary challenge at this level involves building basic awareness. Technical teams often don't recognize AI-specific vulnerabilities. Management may not understand why traditional security proves insufficient. Budget and headcount remain constrained because value hasn't been demonstrated.

Moving beyond Level 1 requires executive sponsorship. Without leadership commitment, security remains an afterthought rather than a core consideration for the organization. Small wins can help build momentum. Preventing a single high-profile incident can catalyze organizational investment.

Level 2: Developing Practices

Organizations at this level have begun implementing systematic AI security practices, but still lack consistency and maturity. Some projects adhere to security best practices, whereas others do not. Documentation exists but may be incomplete, outdated, or even an afterthought. Roles and responsibilities are defined, but not universally adopted or respected.

Characteristics include documented security requirements for AI projects, basic threat modeling during design, some adversarial testing before deployment, designated security points of contact for AI teams, and initial developer training programs. Progress is visible but uneven across the organization.

The key challenge at Level 2 involves scaling effective practices. What works for one team may not transfer to others. Competing priorities create pressure to skip security steps. Measuring effectiveness remains difficult without clear metrics.

Organizations can progress by standardizing processes. Develop templates, checklists, and tools that facilitate security. Build communities of practice where teams share lessons learned. Establish metrics that track both leading indicators (completed activities) and lagging indicators (prevented incidents).

Level 3: Defined and Managed

Organizations at this level have established comprehensive AI security programs with clear governance, standard processes, and measurable outcomes. Security is integrated into development workflows rather than bolted on afterward. Most teams consistently understand and follow established practices.

Characteristics include comprehensive AI security policies covering the entire lifecycle, standardized secure development practices applied across teams, regular security assessments with documented findings, a dedicated AI security team providing expertise and oversight, integration with the enterprise security architecture, metrics to track security posture and trends, and regular training and awareness programs. The organization can confidently describe its security approach to regulators and customers.

Challenges at Level 3 center on maintaining momentum and adapting to change. Processes can become bureaucratic, slowing innovation. Teams may treat security as a checkbox rather than a genuine risk reduction. The evolution of the threat landscape requires continuous process updates.

Progress requires embedding security into culture. Make security everyone's responsibility, not just the security team's job. Recognize and reward good security practices. Establish feedback loops in which security findings drive process improvements. Balance rigor with agility so security enables rather than impedes innovation within the organization.

Level 4: Measured and Optimizing

Organizations at this level continuously improve security through data-driven decision-making and optimization. They actively track leading indicators, analyze trends, and adjust strategies based on evidence. Security innovation happens systematically rather than sporadically.

Characteristics include quantitative security metrics to inform resource allocation, continuous improvement processes driven by data analysis, proactive threat hunting to identify issues before exploitation, automated security testing integrated throughout development, regular benchmarking against industry best practices, contributions to industry standards and knowledge sharing, and predictive analytics to forecast emerging risks. These organizations set the standard others aspire to reach.

Maintaining Level 4 maturity requires investment and leadership commitment. Complacency represents a constant threat. Yesterday's cutting-edge practices become tomorrow's table stakes. Organizations must balance optimization with innovation, refining existing capabilities while exploring new approaches.

The goal extends beyond protecting your own organization. Level 4 organizations advance the field through knowledge sharing, standards development, tool development, and community building. Their security innovations ripple across the industry.

Assessing Your Organization

Self-assessment provides the starting point for maturity improvement. Honest evaluation of current capabilities, identification of gaps, and prioritization of enhancements enable systematic progress. Several assessment approaches prove valuable.

Structured questionnaires evaluate capabilities across multiple dimensions. Cover technical practices (threat modeling, secure coding, testing), organizational factors (governance, resources, training), and cultural elements (awareness, accountability, collaboration). Score each dimension and aggregate the scores to obtain an overall maturity rating.

Benchmarking comparisons reveal how your organization compares with peers. Industry surveys provide external reference points. Be realistic about comparisons. Organizations at different AI maturity levels need different security maturity levels. A company beginning its AI journey doesn't require the same level of security sophistication as a tech giant that is deploying AI at scale.

Gap analysis identifies specific improvement opportunities. List desired capabilities for your target maturity level. Compare against the current state. Prioritize gaps based on risk exposure and implementation feasibility. Create roadmaps with concrete milestones and success criteria.

Independent assessments provide external validation and fresh perspectives. Engage third-party experts to audit your AI security practices. Their experience across multiple organizations reveals blind spots and identifies opportunities for optimization. External validation also carries weight with executives and boards.

Building Maturity Systematically

Maturity improvement requires a deliberate strategy rather than random activity. Several principles guide effective maturity building.

Start with Fundamentals

Master the basics before pursuing the advanced capabilities. Ensure you have comprehensive asset inventories before implementing sophisticated monitoring. Establish clear policies before building complex enforcement mechanisms. Get the foundation right before adding layers.

Organizations often want to skip Level 4 capabilities. This usually fails. Advanced practices depend on foundational elements. Skipping levels creates unstable security programs vulnerable to regression under pressure.

Align with Business Value

Security maturity must deliver business value. Connect security improvements to business outcomes such as faster time-to-market, reduced incident costs, improved customer trust, or regulatory compliance. Quantify value where possible to justify continued investment.

Frame security as an enabler of innovation rather than a barrier. Mature security practices accelerate development by identifying issues early when they're cheapest to fix. Compliance-ready systems expand market opportunities. Robust security becomes a competitive advantage.

Engage Stakeholders

AI security requires collaboration among technical teams, business units, legal and compliance teams, and executive leadership. Build coalitions of support. Educate stakeholders about risks and mitigation strategies. Create forums for ongoing dialogue and coordination.

Different stakeholders need different messages. Executives care about business risk and competitive positioning. Engineers want practical tools and clear requirements. Compliance teams focus on regulatory obligations. Tailor communication while maintaining consistent core messaging.

Measure and Communicate Progress

Establish metrics tracking to measure maturity improvement over time. Celebrate milestones publicly. Share success stories demonstrating security value. Use data to guide resource allocation and prioritize next investments.

Metrics should span technical, organizational, and business dimensions. Track vulnerability trends, coverage of security practices, training completion rates, time to detect and respond to issues, and business impact of security improvements. Balanced scorecards prevent gaming any single metric.

Embed Continuous Improvement

Maturity building never finishes. The threat landscape evolves. Technology advances. Organizational needs change. Build improvement into standard processes through regular reviews, post-incident analysis, benchmarking exercises, and experimentation.

Create dedicated time and resources for improvement. If security teams spend 100% of their time on reactive work, they cannot invest in capability building. Reserve capacity for strategic initiatives that enhance long-term effectiveness.

8.2 The Evolving Standards and Regulatory Ecosystem

Standards Landscape

AI security standards are rapidly maturing from early drafts to implemented frameworks. Understanding the standards landscape helps organizations align their practices with emerging requirements and avoid reinventing the wheel.

International Standards Organizations

ISO/IEC Joint Technical Committee 1 leads international standards development for AI. ISO/IEC 23894 provides guidance on risk management for AI systems. ISO/IEC 5338 addresses AI lifecycle management. ISO/IEC 24028 offers trustworthiness frameworks. These standards provide high-level principles applicable across industries and jurisdictions.

The advantage of ISO standards lies in international recognition and broad applicability. The challenge involves generality. These frameworks require significant interpretation and customization for specific contexts. They establish baseline expectations rather than detailed implementation guidance.

NIST (National Institute of Standards and Technology) publishes influential frameworks and guidance despite being U.S.-focused. The NIST AI Risk Management Framework provides a practical structure for identifying and addressing AI risks. NIST Special Publications provide detailed technical guidance on topics such as adversarial robustness and privacy preservation.

Industry-Specific Standards

Vertical industries are developing sector-specific AI security standards reflecting unique risks and regulatory environments.

Healthcare standards address privacy, safety, and bias concerns. FDA guidance on medical device cybersecurity increasingly covers AI-enabled systems. HL7 FHIR specifications incorporate AI transparency requirements. DICOM standards for medical imaging include provisions for metadata for AI algorithms.

Financial services standards focus on explainability, fairness, and resilience. The Monetary Authority of Singapore published comprehensive AI governance frameworks. Federal Reserve guidance addresses model risk management for AI. Industry groups like FINOS create open standards for financial AI.

Automotive standards emphasize functional safety and security. ISO 21434 addresses cybersecurity engineering for road vehicles, including AI components. UNECE WP.29 regulations mandate the implementation of cybersecurity management systems. ANSI/UL 4600 provides safety frameworks for autonomous systems.

Open Standards and Frameworks

Community-developed standards often move faster than formal standards bodies. Several open frameworks have gained significant adoption.

The MLCommons AI Safety Working Group develops benchmarks for evaluating AI system safety. These benchmarks enable objective comparison and track field progress over time. Public leaderboards create transparency and motivate improvement.

OpenSSF (Open Source Security Foundation) extends software security best practices to machine learning. Scorecards evaluate repository security. SLSA (Supply-chain Levels for Software Artifacts) frameworks apply to ML artifacts such as models and datasets.

OWASP (Open Web Application Security Project) maintains the Top 10 for Large Language Models and the Machine Learning Security Top 10. These lists raise awareness about common vulnerabilities and drive industry focus toward high-impact issues.

Regulatory Evolution

AI regulation is rapidly transitioning from proposals to enforceable requirements. The regulatory landscape varies significantly across jurisdictions but shows clear trends toward comprehensive frameworks.

European Union Leadership

The EU AI Act represents the most comprehensive AI regulation to date. It establishes a risk-based framework categorizing AI systems from minimal to unacceptable risk. High-risk systems require substantial risk management, data governance, transparency, human oversight, and accuracy.

The Act requires conformity assessments before deployment, ongoing monitoring, and incident reporting. Penalties for non-compliance reach €30 million or 6% of global revenue. While initially focused on EU deployment, the Act's extraterritorial effects create de facto global standards similar to GDPR's impact.

GDPR continues evolving through enforcement actions and regulatory guidance. The right to explanation for automated decisions, data minimization principles, and purpose limitation requirements all constrain the design and operation of AI systems. Recent rulings address issues like algorithmic discrimination and automated decision-making.

The United States Approach

The U.S. takes a more fragmented sectoral approach rather than comprehensive federal legislation. The AI Bill of Rights provides high-level principles but lacks enforcement mechanisms. Various agencies address AI within their jurisdictions.

The FTC (Federal Trade Commission) uses its existing consumer protection authority to address AI issues such as algorithmic discrimination and deceptive practices. Enforcement actions against biased algorithms and inadequate security set practical precedents.

EEOC (Equal Employment Opportunity Commission) scrutinizes AI in hiring for discrimination. Guidance requires employers to audit automated systems for bias and provide reasonable accommodations when AI disadvantages protected groups.

FDA regulates AI in medical devices through premarket review and postmarket surveillance. The agency is developing frameworks for continuously learning systems that update after deployment, addressing unique AI challenges.

State-level regulation fills federal gaps. California, Colorado, and other states passed AI transparency and accountability laws. This creates compliance complexity as requirements vary across jurisdictions.

Asia-Pacific Developments

China implemented comprehensive AI regulation through multiple frameworks. Personal Information Protection Law (PIPL) imposes strict data governance requirements. Algorithmic Recommendation Management Provisions mandate transparency in recommendation systems. Deep Synthesis Management Provisions address generative AI.

Singapore takes a more principles-based approach through the Model AI Governance Framework. This emphasizes risk management and accountability while avoiding prescriptive requirements. The strategy seeks to balance innovation with consumer protection.

Japan focuses on soft law and industry self-regulation. Guidelines and best practices provide direction without legal mandates. This approach prioritizes flexibility but may prove less effective at addressing harmful practices.

Navigating Regulatory Complexity

Multi-jurisdictional operations face complex compliance requirements. Several strategies help manage this complexity.

Adopt the Highest Standard

Design systems to meet the most stringent applicable requirements. If operating in both the EU and the U.S., build to EU AI Act standards. This simplifies compliance and eliminates the need to maintain separate versions for different markets.

The risk involves potential over-engineering and competitive disadvantage versus local-only competitors. Weigh compliance simplification against implementation costs. For many organizations, unified standards prove more cost-effective than fragmented approaches.

Implement Compliance by Design

Integrate regulatory requirements into development processes rather than retrofitting compliance later. Build privacy protections, bias testing, and explainability into standard workflows. Make compliance natural rather than exceptional.

Compliance by design reduces costs and risks. Finding compliance gaps during development costs far less than post-deployment remediation. It also reduces regulatory risk from non-compliant systems operating in production.

Maintain Regulatory Intelligence

Track regulatory developments systematically. Subscribe to regulatory updates from relevant jurisdictions. Participate in industry associations sharing regulatory intelligence. Engage regulatory experts who specialize in AI governance.

Build internal processes for assessing regulatory impact and cascading changes through the organization. Designate owners responsible for monitoring specific regulations. Create cross-functional forums where legal, compliance, and technical teams coordinate responses.

Engage Regulators Proactively

Many regulatory agencies welcome engagement with regulated entities. Participate in comment periods for proposed regulations. Request advance rulings on novel situations. Build relationships with regulatory staff.

Proactive engagement serves multiple purposes. It helps shape regulations before they solidify into potentially unworkable requirements. It demonstrates a good faith effort at compliance. It creates channels for ongoing dialogue as issues arise.

8.3 Building Effective AI Security Programs

Program Foundations

Effective AI security programs require proper foundations spanning governance, resources, processes, and culture. Each element contributes to overall program effectiveness.

Governance Structure

Clear governance establishes authority, accountability, and decision-making processes. Who sets AI security policy? Who approves exceptions? Who owns incident response? Answering these questions before crises arise prevents chaos and confusion.

Governance models vary based on organizational structure and culture. Centralized models vest authority in a dedicated AI security team. Decentralized models distribute responsibility across business units or product teams with coordination from a central office. Hybrid approaches combine elements of both.

Most organizations benefit from hybrid governance. Central teams establish standards, provide expertise, and coordinate across the organization. Local teams implement security appropriate to their contexts and business needs. Cross-functional governance boards resolve conflicts and prioritize initiatives.

The governance structure should align with the overall organizational design. Don't create AI security governance that conflicts with how the organization actually makes decisions. Work within existing frameworks while adapting them for AI-specific needs.

Resource Allocation

AI security requires dedicated resources, including people, tools, and budget. Resource constraints force prioritization and trade-offs. Effective programs allocate resources based on risk and business value rather than squeaky wheels or politics.

Staffing represents the most critical resource. AI security requires rare combinations of security expertise and AI knowledge. Build these capabilities through hiring, training existing staff, or supplementing internal teams with external expertise.

Don't expect to hire your way to complete coverage. The talent market remains highly constrained. Develop internal expertise through training programs, rotations, and mentorship. Create career paths that retain developed talent.

Tools and infrastructure enable security at scale. Automated testing tools, monitoring platforms, model governance systems, and secure development environments all require investment. Build versus buy decisions depend on organizational context, but most organizations benefit from commercial tools supplemented with custom solutions for unique needs.

Process Design

Processes translate strategy into repeatable actions. Effective AI security processes integrate seamlessly into development workflows rather than creating separate tracks that developers tend to avoid.

Design processes should be lightweight and practical. Security processes that impose significant overhead without clear value get circumvented. Focus on essential controls that genuinely reduce risk. Automate wherever possible to reduce manual burden.

Build flexibility into processes for varying risk contexts. High-stakes applications warrant more rigorous security reviews than low-risk experiments. Risk-based approaches allocate effort proportional to potential impact.

Document processes clearly with templates, checklists, and examples. Make it easy for teams to do the right thing. Provide self-service tools and resources so teams can proceed without waiting for centralized reviews except where truly necessary.

Cultural Elements

Security culture determines whether policies are followed and processes are used. Culture change requires sustained effort and leadership reinforcement.

Make security psychologically safe. Teams should feel comfortable raising concerns and reporting issues without fear of punishment.

Blameless post-mortems focus on system improvements rather than individual failures. Recognition and rewards reinforce positive behaviors.

Integrate security into engineering excellence. Frame security as a quality attribute, alongside performance and reliability. Make security expertise a valued specialization. Include security contributions in performance evaluations and promotion criteria.

Build security champions within product teams. Designate and train individuals who become local experts and advocates. Champions bridge the gap between central security teams and distributed development, translating generic guidance into context-specific practices.

Program Components

Comprehensive AI security programs include multiple interconnected components spanning the AI lifecycle.

Policy and Standards

Written policies establish expectations and requirements. Effective policies balance clarity with flexibility. Overly prescriptive policies become outdated quickly. Overly vague policies provide insufficient guidance.

AI security policies should address key topics, including acceptable use of AI systems, data governance for training and evaluation, model development and testing requirements, deployment approval processes, monitoring and incident response, third-party AI services, and AI supply chain security.

Standards provide detailed technical requirements for implementing policy objectives. While policies answer "what" and "why," standards answer "how." Standards evolve more frequently than policies as technology and threats change.

Maintain policy and standards in accessible locations with clear version control. Policies buried on intranet sites don't influence behavior. Make them discoverable and understandable. Supplement with FAQs, examples, and decision trees.

Risk Assessment

Systematic risk assessment identifies threats, vulnerabilities, and potential impacts. Risk assessments guide resource allocation and prioritization. They also demonstrate due diligence to both regulators and stakeholders.

AI risk assessments should address traditional security risks as well as AI-specific concerns. Consider adversarial examples, data poisoning, model extraction, privacy violations, bias and discrimination, safety failures, and emerging threats specific to your use cases.

Risk assessment methodologies range from qualitative to quantitative. Qualitative approaches use scales like low/medium/high risk. Quantitative methods estimate probabilities and impacts numerically. Most organizations start with qualitative approaches and add quantification for critical systems.

Conduct initial risk assessments during system design and repeat periodically throughout the lifecycle. Trigger reassessments when systems change significantly, new threats emerge, or incidents occur. Document assessments and track risk mitigation actions.

Secure Development Practices

Development practices directly determine system security. Secure development for AI extends traditional practices with AI-specific considerations.

Threat modeling during design identifies potential attacks before implementation. Model the system architecture, enumerate threat actors and their capabilities, identify attack surfaces and vectors, and analyze potential impacts. Use frameworks like STRIDE or MITRE ATT&CK to structure analysis.

Security testing throughout development catches vulnerabilities early when they're cheapest to fix. Combine multiple testing approaches, including adversarial robustness testing, fairness and bias evaluation, privacy analysis, input validation testing, and dependency scanning.

Code review catches security issues during development. Train reviewers on AI-specific vulnerabilities. Use checklists covering common issues. Consider a security-focused review for high-risk changes.

Dependency management addresses supply chain risks. Many AI systems rely on third-party frameworks, pre-trained models, and datasets. Validate dependencies, monitor for vulnerabilities, and establish update processes.

Deployment Controls

Deployment represents a critical control point. Inappropriate deployment decisions create lasting security impacts. Effective deployment controls balance security with development velocity.

Approval processes ensure systems meet security requirements before production deployment. Tailor approval rigor to risk levels. High-stakes systems warrant a formal security review. Lower-risk systems might use automated checks with exception handling.

Deployment checklists ensure consistent evaluation. Cover security testing completion, risk assessment documentation, monitoring configuration, incident response preparation, regulatory compliance, and stakeholder approval. Make checklists readily available and easy to complete.

Phased rollouts reduce risk from unknown issues. Deploy initially to a limited set of users or use cases. Monitor carefully for problems. Expand gradually as confidence builds. Maintain rollback capabilities if issues emerge.

Monitoring and Detection

Production monitoring detects attacks, misuse, and degradation. Effective monitoring combines automated detection with human analysis.

Monitor multiple dimensions, including input distributions for drift detection, output distributions for unexpected patterns, model performance for accuracy degradation, adversarial indicators like evasion attempts, privacy metrics for data leakage risks, fairness metrics for bias emergence, and system health for availability and reliability.

Establish baselines during normal operation. Detect anomalies by comparing current behavior against baselines. Update baselines as systems and environments evolve to avoid false alarms.

Alert design determines monitoring effectiveness. Too many alerts cause fatigue, and important signals get missed. Too few alerts miss genuine issues. Tune alerting carefully based on operational experience.

Incident Response

Despite preventive measures, security incidents will occur. Effective incident response limits damage and enables rapid recovery.

Incident response plans define procedures for detection, analysis, containment, eradication, recovery, and lessons learned. Plans should address AI-specific scenarios such as adversarial attacks, data poisoning detection, and model extraction.

Response teams need clear roles and responsibilities. Who leads the response? Who communicates with the stakeholders? Who analyzes the incident? Who implements fixes? Define these roles before incidents create confusion.

Practice incident response through tabletop exercises and simulations. Simulated incidents reveal procedural gaps and improve team coordination without the stress of real events. Schedule regular exercises and update plans based on lessons learned.

Post-incident analysis drives improvement. Conduct blameless reviews focusing on systemic issues rather than individual errors. Identify root causes and contributing factors. Implement corrective actions to prevent recurrence.

Program Evolution

Security programs must evolve as organizations, technologies, and threats change. Static programs quickly become obsolete and ineffective.

Establish regular program reviews to assess effectiveness and identify improvements. Reviews should consider metrics and trends, incident patterns and lessons learned, emerging threats and vulnerabilities, technology and architecture changes, regulatory developments, and benchmark comparisons. Incorporate continuous improvement processes. Assign ownership for specific improvement initiatives. Track progress systematically. Celebrate successes to maintain momentum.

Balance operational demands with strategic improvement. Reserve capacity for enhancement rather than spending 100% of resources on reactive work. Strategic investments in automation, tooling, and capability building pay dividends through improved efficiency and effectiveness.

8.4 Cross-Functional Collaboration

The Collaboration Imperative

AI security cannot succeed as a purely technical discipline. Effective security requires collaboration across functions, including engineering, product management, legal, compliance, human resources, and executive leadership. Each brings essential perspectives and capabilities.

Breaking down silos represents one of the biggest organizational challenges. Technical teams, business units, and support functions often operate independently with limited coordination. AI security demands integration.

Key Stakeholder Groups

Engineering and Data Science

Technical teams build and maintain AI systems. They implement security controls, conduct testing, and respond to technical issues. Security must enable their work rather than obstruct it.

Effective collaboration with technical teams requires understanding their constraints and motivations. Engineers want to ship products quickly. They resist processes that slow development without clear value. Security must demonstrate value and minimize friction.

Embed security expertise within development teams rather than creating separate security silos. Security champions within teams understand both security principles and development realities. They translate generic security guidance into practical implementations.

Provide tools and automation that make secure development easier. Static analysis catching vulnerabilities during development costs less than manual reviews. Automated testing enables continuous security validation. Self-service security resources let teams proceed without waiting.

Product and Business Teams

Product managers and business leaders make decisions about features, timelines, and resource allocation. They often lack deep security expertise but are still held responsible for product success.

Security must communicate in business terms. Translate technical risks into business impacts. Quantify potential costs from security failures. Frame security controls as enabling capabilities rather than constraints. Involve security early in product planning. Security retrofitted after design proves more expensive and less effective than security by design. Early involvement also builds relationships and trust.

Balance security with other priorities. Perfect security might be impossible or prohibitively expensive. Help product teams make informed risk decisions rather than insisting on absolute security. Provide options with clear tradeoffs.

Legal and Compliance

Legal and compliance teams ensure regulatory adherence and manage legal risks. They interpret requirements and establish acceptable practices. Security and compliance teams share common goals but sometimes clash over approaches. Compliance focuses on meeting minimum requirements. Security aims to reduce risk beyond regulatory mandates. Both perspectives provide value.

Establish regular coordination between security and compliance. Joint reviews of new regulations identify overlapping requirements and avoid duplicate efforts. Collaborative risk assessments leverage both security and legal expertise.

Compliance requirements can drive security improvements. Regulatory mandates often justify investments that security teams struggled to obtain through risk arguments alone. Frame security initiatives in compliance terms when beneficial.

Executive Leadership

Executive commitment determines program success. Without leadership support, security initiatives lack the resources and authority to succeed. With strong support, security becomes an organizational priority.

Communicate with executives in their language. Board and C-suite care about business risk, competitive positioning, regulatory exposure, and reputation. Technical details matter less than business implications.

Provide regular briefings on security posture, emerging threats, and program progress. Make these briefings concise and actionable. Focus on the decisions executives must make rather than the information they might find interesting.

Escalate appropriately when security concerns require leadership attention. Don't cry wolf over minor issues. Reserve escalation for genuine business risks. Provide clear recommendations rather than just describing problems.

Collaboration Mechanisms

Effective collaboration requires structured mechanisms, not just good intentions.

Cross-Functional Forums

Regular meetings with representatives from key stakeholder groups provide coordination and communication. Use these forums to share information about threats and incidents, discuss emerging technologies and approaches, resolve conflicts between competing priorities, align on strategic direction, and build relationships across organizational boundaries.

Keep forums focused and productive. Establish clear agendas. Document decisions and action items. Follow up on commitments. Avoid letting forums become places for information sharing without decision-making.

Working Groups

Dedicated working groups address specific initiatives or problems. Working groups provide deeper collaboration than broad forums enable. They develop expertise and drive sustained progress on complex issues.

Form working groups around specific topics like bias mitigation strategies, privacy-preserving techniques, supply chain security, or regulatory compliance. Include relevant expertise from across the organization. Set clear objectives and timelines. Ensure working groups produce tangible outputs. Deliverables might include technical standards, process documentation, tool evaluations, or pilot project results. Outputs justify the time investment and create lasting value.

Embedded Partnerships

Embedding security experts within business units creates tight collaboration. Embedded security engineers work alongside development teams, understanding their context and building trust through daily interaction.

Embedded models work best when security experts maintain connections to central security teams. This balances context-specific knowledge with consistent practices and shared learning across the organization.

Consider rotational programs where security experts spend time embedded with different teams. Rotations build broad organizational knowledge and create networks spanning silos.

Communication Channels

Establish clear communication channels for different types of interactions. Dedicated Slack channels, email lists, or collaboration platforms facilitate ongoing discussion. Make it easy for any team member to ask security questions or report concerns.

Balance accessibility with signal-to-noise ratio. Open channels that anyone can post in may become chaotic. Moderated channels with clear purposes maintain focus. Different channels serve different needs, from urgent escalations to general questions.

Building Collaborative Culture

Mechanisms alone don't guarantee effective collaboration. Cultural factors determine whether collaboration actually happens.

Mutual Respect

Security teams must respect the expertise and constraints of other functions. Developers understand implementation realities that security specialists might miss. Business teams grasp market and customer dynamics. Legal teams interpret regulatory requirements.

Similarly, other teams should respect security expertise. Security professionals study attacker techniques, understand vulnerabilities, and track emerging threats. Their concerns reflect real risks, not paranoia. Mutual respect enables productive dialogue. Teams listen to one another, consider different perspectives, and find solutions that balance multiple priorities.

Shared Objectives

Align on common goals transcending individual functions. Everyone wants successful products, satisfied customers, regulatory compliance, and organizational success. Security enables these shared objectives rather than conflicting with them.

Frame security in terms of shared objectives. Security improvements reduce customer churn from breaches. Robust systems enable market expansion into regulated industries. Secure development accelerates time-to-market by finding issues early.

Transparency

Share information openly within appropriate boundaries. Security teams should explain threats, vulnerabilities, and defensive strategies. Other teams should share plans, constraints, and concerns. Transparency builds trust and enables better decisions.

Balance transparency with confidentiality. Some security information shouldn't be widely shared if it could benefit attackers. Some business information remains proprietary. Establish clear guidelines for information handling.

Recognition

Recognize and reward collaborative behavior. Public acknowledgment of teams working effectively across functions reinforces the desired culture. Include collaboration in performance evaluations and promotion criteria.

Celebrate successes that demonstrate collaboration value for the organization. When security and engineering teams collaborate to prevent an attack or to launch a secure product, publicize the achievement. Success stories motivate continued collaboration.

8.5 Long-Term Trends Shaping AI Security

Technology Evolution

Several long-term technology trends will fundamentally reshape AI security over the coming decade.

Foundation Model Proliferation

Foundation models trained on massive datasets and fine-tuned for specific tasks are becoming the norm rather than the exception. This shift creates new security dynamics. Concentration of training in a few organizations creates systemic risk. If major foundation model providers suffer security compromises, the impacts ripple across entire ecosystems. Diversification of foundation model sources mitigates but doesn't eliminate these risks.

Fine-tuning and adaptation become primary development activities rather than training from scratch. Security must address fine-tuning attacks, adapter security, and prompt injection. Traditional training-time defenses prove insufficient.

Model marketplaces and model-as-a-service platforms expand attack surfaces. Malicious models, watermark removal, and unauthorized fine-tuning create new threat vectors. Secure model distribution and usage verification become critical capabilities.

Multimodal Integration

AI systems increasingly process and generate multiple modalities, including text, images, audio, video, and sensor data. Multimodal systems create richer functionality but also expanded attack surfaces.

Cross-modal attacks exploit interactions between modalities. Adversarial images might trigger harmful text generation. Seemingly benign text could cause dangerous image synthesis. Defenses must consider cross-modal effects rather than securing each modality independently.

Multimodal models require more complex testing and validation. Security evaluation must cover all supported modalities and their combinations. Test suites expand dramatically compared to single-modality systems.

Agentic AI Systems

AI systems are evolving from tools that respond to queries toward agents that pursue goals autonomously. Agentic systems make decisions, take actions, and interact with environments with reduced human oversight. Goal misalignment becomes more consequential in agentic systems. Misspecified objectives or reward hacking can cause unintended, harmful behaviors. Ensuring robust alignment at design time and monitoring for misalignment during operation both prove essential.

Agentic systems interact with APIs, databases, and physical systems. These interactions create novel attack vectors. Prompt injection might cause agents to execute unauthorized database operations. Adversarial manipulation could cause harmful physical actions.

Human oversight and intervention mechanisms become safety-critical features. Agentic systems need safeguards enabling humans to intervene when systems behave unexpectedly. Designing effective oversight without eliminating autonomy benefits poses significant challenges.

Quantum Computing

While practical large-scale quantum computers remain years away, their eventual arrival will fundamentally disrupt cryptographic security.

Current public-key cryptography will become vulnerable to quantum attacks. Organizations must begin transitioning to quantum-resistant algorithms before quantum computers achieve sufficient scale. This transition requires years of planning and implementation.

Adversaries might employ "harvest now, decrypt later" strategies, collecting encrypted AI model updates, training data, and communications for future decryption when quantum computers become available. Protecting long-lived secrets requires quantum-resistant cryptography today.

Quantum computing might also enable new AI capabilities and vulnerabilities. Quantum machine learning algorithms could provide performance advantages. They might also create new attack vectors or defensive capabilities. Research continues exploring these possibilities.

Threat Evolution

The threat landscape will evolve in parallel with technology advancements.

Industrialized Attacks

AI attacks are transitioning from research demonstrations to practical exploits and eventually to industrialized attack infrastructure. Attack-as-a-service platforms will emerge, enabling less sophisticated adversaries to conduct advanced attacks.

Automated attack tools will reduce skill barriers. Current adversarial attacks require machine learning expertise. Future tools might enable attacks with simple interfaces and minimal knowledge. Defensive capabilities must scale accordingly.

AI systems will attack other AI systems. Generative models might automatically discover adversarial examples. Reinforcement learning might optimize data poisoning strategies. Attack automation increases both speed and sophistication.

Nation-State Capabilities

Nation-state actors are investing heavily in AI attack capabilities. These adversaries combine technical sophistication with substantial resources and long time horizons.

Supply chain attacks will increase as nation-states target AI infrastructure. Compromised training data, backdoored models, and malicious frameworks create persistent footholds. International supply chains complicate detection and attribution.

AI-enabled disinformation campaigns will become more sophisticated. Generative models creating convincing fake content combine with targeting algorithms and automated distribution. Defending information ecosystems requires technical and policy innovations.

Cyber-physical attacks leveraging AI vulnerabilities could have severe consequences. Manipulation of autonomous vehicles, industrial control systems, or medical devices might cause physical harm. Security must consider worst-case scenarios in high-stakes domains.

Insider Threats

AI development attracts insider threats by concentrating valuable intellectual property and sensitive data. Model theft by departing employees or contractors costs organizations their competitive advantage. Insider access to training systems and model repositories creates opportunities for exfiltration. Technical controls that limit access and detect abnormal activity provide some protection.

Sabotage of AI systems through data poisoning or backdoor insertion is difficult to detect, particularly when perpetrated by trusted insiders with legitimate access. Defense in depth, code review, and behavioral monitoring mitigate these risks but don't eliminate them.

Inadvertent insider errors will continue to cause security issues. Misconfigurations exposing training data, accidental deployment of vulnerable models, and improper access controls create exploitable vulnerabilities. Security must account for human error.

Societal Developments

Broader societal trends will shape AI security beyond purely technical dimensions.

Regulatory Maturity

AI regulation will mature from principles and guidelines to detailed requirements and active enforcement. Organizations must prepare for increasing compliance burdens.

Regulatory fragmentation across jurisdictions will create complexity. Different regions will adopt varying approaches to AI governance. Multinational organizations must navigate this complexity through unified standards that meet the highest requirements or jurisdiction-specific implementations.

Enforcement actions will provide clarity through precedent. Early enforcement will test regulatory boundaries and establish practical interpretations. Organizations should monitor enforcement closely to understand regulator expectations. Industry self-regulation might prevent or delay government mandates. Proactive adoption of standards and best practices demonstrates responsibility. Effective self-regulation requires accountability mechanisms and consequences for violations.

Public Awareness and Expectations

Public awareness of AI risks is increasing through media coverage, incidents, and education. Rising awareness creates pressure for improved security and accountability.

Customer expectations for AI security will increase. Organizations with poor security track records might face customer backlash and competitive disadvantage. Security becomes a market differentiator. Algorithmic accountability movements will demand transparency and contestability. Users will expect to understand how AI systems affect them and to challenge unfair decisions. Technical and procedural mechanisms for explainability and appeal become necessary.

Privacy concerns will intensify as AI systems collect and process an expanding range of data types. Privacy-preserving techniques transition from research novelties to market requirements. Organizations failing to protect privacy face regulatory and reputational consequences.

Talent Development

The AI security talent shortage will gradually ease but will remain a constraint for years. Multiple strategies address this challenge. Educational institutions are developing AI security curricula. University programs, bootcamps, and certification courses are emerging. Standardized curricula improve baseline knowledge but don't eliminate the need for organizational training.

Industry training and upskilling programs enable career transitions. Security professionals can add AI expertise. AI engineers can develop security knowledge. Cross-training builds the interdisciplinary skills AI security requires.

Tool improvements reduce expertise requirements for some tasks. Automated adversarial testing, bias-detection platforms, and security-aware development environments enable less specialized practitioners to implement best practices. Expertise still proves necessary for novel challenges.

8.6 Preparing for the Future

Strategic Positioning

Organizations should position themselves strategically for AI security's evolving landscape.

Invest in Foundations

Build strong foundations spanning people, processes, and technology. Foundational capabilities prove valuable regardless of how specific threats evolve. Threat modeling, secure development, and incident response remain relevant even as attack techniques change.

Prioritize fundamentals over bleeding-edge techniques. Master adversarial training before pursuing exotic defenses. Establish comprehensive data governance before implementing complex privacy techniques. Strong foundations support advanced capabilities.

Maintain Flexibility

Avoid over-commitment to specific technologies or approaches. The field evolves rapidly. Today's best practices might become tomorrow's anti-patterns. Build adaptability into programs and architectures.

Design security architectures for evolution. Modular designs enable the replacement of specific components without system-wide overhauls. Abstract interfaces separate security mechanisms from their implementations.

Budget for experimentation and innovation. Reserve resources for exploring emerging techniques and technologies. Pilot programs enable learning without full commitment. Successful pilots justify broader adoption.

Build Ecosystems

Participate actively in the broader AI security ecosystem. Ecosystem engagement provides multiple benefits, including early warning of emerging threats, access to shared tools and resources, opportunities for collaboration, and influence on evolving standards.

Contribute to open-source security tools and frameworks. Open-source accelerates field progress and facilitates shared infrastructure. Contributing builds reputation and influence while improving the tools you use.

Participate in industry working groups and standards bodies. Standards work shapes future requirements. Early participation enables influence over the content of standards. Implementation experience informs better standards.

Engage in information-sharing communities. Threat intelligence, incident lessons learned, and defensive best practices benefit all participants. Confidentiality concerns can be addressed through anonymization and trust frameworks.

Cultivate Culture

Organizational culture determines long-term security success more than any specific technology or technique. Foster security consciousness across the organization. Security awareness shouldn't be limited to security teams.

Everyone who develops, deploys, or uses AI systems should understand basic security principles and their role in security.

Reward learning and improvement over perfection. Security mistakes will happen. Organizations that punish mistakes drive them underground. Organizations that learn from mistakes and improve processes achieve better outcomes.

Balance security with innovation. Organizations that sacrifice all security for speed eventually face consequences. Organizations that sacrifice all innovation for security become irrelevant. Finding the right balance requires judgment, communication, and continuous adjustment.

Personal Development

Individual security practitioners should also prepare for the field's evolution.

Develop T-Shaped Expertise

Build both depth and breadth in your knowledge. Depth in specific areas, such as adversarial robustness or privacy-preserving ML, enables technical contributions. Breadth across security, AI, and related fields enables effective collaboration and architectural thinking. Specialize while maintaining generalist knowledge. Deep expertise provides differentiated value. Broad knowledge enables effective work across specialties and communication with diverse stakeholders.

Follow the 70-20-10 development model. Spend 70% of time on current role and responsibilities. Spend 20% on expanding into adjacent areas. Spend 10% on exploring novel topics that might become important. This balance maintains current effectiveness while building future capabilities.

Build Interdisciplinary Skills

AI security requires combining security expertise with AI knowledge, software engineering, mathematics, and domain understanding. No one person masters everything, but effective practitioners bridge multiple disciplines over time.

Learn enough AI to understand how systems work and where vulnerabilities hide. Security practitioners need sufficient ML knowledge to recognize attack vectors and evaluate defenses. Formal ML education helps, but it isn't strictly necessary to understand. Acquire sufficient security knowledge to think like adversaries. AI practitioners need a security mindset, including an understanding of attacker motivations, capabilities, and techniques. Security fundamentals provide this foundation.

Develop communication skills for technical and non-technical audiences. Explain security risks to executives. Translate regulatory requirements for engineers. Write clearly for diverse readers. Communication skills amplify technical capabilities.

Engage with the Community

Participate actively in the AI security community through conferences, meetups, online forums, and social media. Community engagement accelerates learning and builds professional networks.

Attend conferences and workshops to learn cutting-edge research and meet other practitioners. Major conferences include IEEE Symposium on Security and Privacy, USENIX Security, ACM CCS, ICML, NeurIPS, and specialized AI security workshops.

Contribute to discussions and share knowledge. Write blog posts explaining concepts you've learned. Speak at meetups about your experiences. Answer questions on forums. Teaching reinforces your own understanding while helping others.

Follow researchers and practitioners on social media and professional networks. Twitter, LinkedIn, and specialized platforms surface relevant content and facilitate discussions. Build your network across organizations and specialties.

Maintain Ethical Grounding

AI security raises profound ethical questions about power, privacy, fairness, and autonomy. Develop and maintain strong ethical frameworks guiding your work.

Understand multiple ethical perspectives beyond your own. Different cultures, communities, and individuals hold varying values. Effective AI security respects this diversity while establishing common ground. Question the systems you build and protect. Not all AI applications deserve security support. Some applications might cause net harm regardless of security. Ethical practitioners sometimes say no to technically feasible but ethically problematic work.

Consider impacts on vulnerable populations. AI systems often disproportionately affect marginalized communities. Security work should protect these groups rather than enabling systems that exploit them.

Chapter Summary

This chapter examined the organizational and strategic dimensions of AI security beyond technical implementation. Several key themes emerged.

AI security maturity progresses through defined levels from reactive firefighting to proactive optimization. Organizations benefit from assessing their current maturity, identifying gaps, and systematically building capabilities. Maturity improvement requires sustained investment and leadership commitment.

The standards and regulatory landscape are rapidly maturing. ISO standards, industry frameworks, and government regulations create increasingly specific requirements. Organizations must navigate multi-jurisdictional complexity while contributing to ecosystem development.

Effective AI security programs require strong foundations spanning governance, resources, processes, and culture. Programs must evolve as organizations, technologies, and threats change. Cross-functional collaboration proves essential for program success.

AI security demands collaboration across engineering, product, legal, compliance, and leadership teams. Breaking down silos through structured mechanisms and a collaborative culture enables comprehensive security that addresses technical, regulatory, and business dimensions.

Long-term trends will reshape AI security over the coming decade. The evolution of technology toward foundation models, multimodal systems, and agentic AI creates new security challenges. Threat industrialization and nation-state investment increase adversary capabilities. Regulatory maturity and public awareness raise compliance and market expectations.

Strategic preparation involves investing in foundations, maintaining flexibility, building ecosystem connections, and cultivating a security culture. Individual practitioners should develop T-shaped expertise, build interdisciplinary skills, engage with the community, and maintain ethical grounding.

Key Takeaways

1. AI security maturity progresses through defined levels. Assess your organization realistically, identify gaps, and build capabilities systematically rather than randomly.

2. Standards and regulations are rapidly maturing from voluntary frameworks to enforceable requirements. Stay informed about developments in your jurisdictions and industries.

3. Effective security programs require governance, resources, processes, and culture working together. No single element suffices. Build comprehensive programs addressing all dimensions.

4. Cross-functional collaboration proves essential. AI security cannot succeed as a purely technical discipline. Build partnerships across organizational boundaries.

5. Long-term technology trends toward foundation models, multimodal systems, and autonomous agents will create new security challenges. Prepare by building strong foundations and maintaining flexibility.

6. Threat landscape will evolve toward industrialized attacks, nation-state capabilities, and insider threats. Defensive capabilities must scale accordingly.

7. Regulatory compliance becomes increasingly important as governments move from guidance to enforcement. Build compliance into development processes rather than retrofitting later.

8. Talent development through education, training, and tool improvement will gradually ease current shortages. Invest in developing your own capabilities and growing your team.

9. Ecosystem participation through standards work, open source contribution, and information sharing benefits everyone. Contribute to the field's advancement while benefiting from shared knowledge.

10. Personal development requires building interdisciplinary expertise, engaging with the community, and maintaining ethical grounding. Continuous learning proves essential in this rapidly evolving field.

Reflection Questions

1. What maturity level best describes your organization's current AI security capabilities? What specific actions would move you to the next level? What barriers prevent progression?

2. How well does your organization balance security, innovation, and compliance? Do you lean too heavily toward any dimension at the expense of others? What adjustments would improve balance?

3. Which cross-functional relationships require strengthening? What mechanisms could improve collaboration between security and other teams? What cultural factors help or hinder collaboration?

4. How well-positioned is your organization for emerging trends like foundation models, multimodal AI, and agentic systems? What investments would improve preparedness?

5. What role do you play in the broader AI security ecosystem? How might you contribute to field advancement through knowledge sharing, standards work, or open source contribution?

6. How do you maintain ethical grounding in your AI security work? What frameworks guide your decisions about which systems to build or protect? How do you account for impacts on vulnerable populations?

7. What personal development priorities will prepare you for AI security's evolution? Where should you build depth versus breadth? What interdisciplinary skills require strengthening?

Conclusion: Your Role in AI Security's Future

AI security stands at a critical juncture. Early experimentation gives way to mature practice. Voluntary frameworks become regulatory requirements. Research demonstrations evolve into production exploits. The field demands unprecedented collaboration between security experts, AI researchers, engineers, policymakers, and ethicists. You carry responsibility for shaping this future. The systems you build, secure, evaluate, regulate, or teach about will operate in a world you help create. Your choices ripple through the ecosystem, affecting colleagues, customers, and communities.

This responsibility proves both a burden and an opportunity. The burden lies in the endless vigilance against evolving threats, the complex trade-offs among competing priorities, and the profound ethical questions with no clear answers. The opportunity lies in preventing harm, enabling beneficial AI applications, and contributing to foundational security infrastructure for future generations.

AI security remains young enough that individual contributions matter tremendously. Standards are still being written. Best practices are still being discovered. Tools are still being built. Early-career practitioners can influence field development in ways that are impossible in more mature disciplines. The technical content in previous chapters equipped you with knowledge about threats, defenses, privacy preservation, bias mitigation, and emerging technologies. This final chapter provided strategic context on maturity models, standards, regulations, program development, and future trends. Knowledge without action remains theoretical. Your challenge now is to translate knowledge into practice.

Start where you are. If your organization lacks formal AI security, begin building awareness and basic practices. If you have established programs, focus on optimization and innovation. If you work in research or education, advance the field by creating knowledge and developing talent. Every role contributes to the collective mission of securing AI systems.

Collaborate generously. Share knowledge with colleagues and the community. Contribute to open source tools and standards. Participate in information sharing. Strong AI security requires cooperative efforts beyond the capabilities of any single organization. Think long-term. The systems we build today will operate for decades. Security decisions echo far into the future. Consider not just immediate threats but emerging risks that will materialize years from now. Build foundations enabling adaptation as the landscape evolves.

Maintain ethical commitment. Technical excellence without ethical grounding proves insufficient and potentially dangerous. Question the systems you work on. Consider who benefits and who might be harmed. Advocate for responsible AI development and deployment.

The future of AI security begins now with you, with this knowledge, with this commitment. You are not just learning about AI security. You are shaping its future. Build wisely. Build securely. Build a future where artificial intelligence amplifies human potential while protecting human values and dignity.

The responsibility is heavy. The opportunity is immense. The future awaits your contribution.

9

The Path Forward

Learning Objectives

By the end of this chapter, you will:

- Synthesize key insights from across all aspects of AI security
- Understand the interconnected nature of technical, organizational, and societal challenges
- Recognize your role in shaping AI security's future
- Develop a personal action plan for contributing to secure AI development
- Appreciate both the urgency and the long-term nature of AI security work
- Connect individual actions to collective progress
- Maintain realistic optimism about achieving meaningful security improvements

Introduction: The Synthesis

You have journeyed through the landscape of AI security across eight comprehensive chapters. You explored foundational concepts of AI systems and their unique vulnerabilities. You confronted the adversarial threat landscape in all its complexity. You examined secure development practices, ethical considerations, and regulatory frameworks. You studied defensive techniques, privacy preservation, and emerging technologies. You considered organizational maturity and strategic positioning.

Now comes the crucial step. Knowledge without application remains theoretical. Understanding without action produces no security improvements. This final chapter synthesizes insights from our entire exploration and charts a clear path forward. We examine what this knowledge means for you, your organization, and the broader community working to secure AI systems. The challenges ahead are formidable. AI capabilities advance faster than our understanding of security. Adversaries grow more sophisticated. Regulatory requirements increase in complexity. Perfect security remains impossible. Yet despite these challenges, meaningful progress is achievable through sustained, coordinated effort.

This chapter is not about summarizing what came before. It is about transforming understanding into action, converting knowledge into commitment, and channeling individual efforts toward collective progress. The future of AI security depends on what we do next.

9.1 The Essential Synthesis

Interconnected Challenges

AI security cannot be understood as isolated technical problems requiring isolated technical solutions. The challenges we face interconnect across multiple dimensions, creating a complex system where actions in one area ripple through others.

Technical Interdependencies

Adversarial robustness connects to privacy preservation. Techniques that make models robust against adversarial examples often require additional training data or computational resources, potentially conflicting with differential privacy constraints. Defending against membership inference attacks through differential privacy can reduce adversarial robustness. Trade-offs require careful navigation.

Model interpretability relates to security testing. Explainable models enable more effective security analysis because humans can understand decision-making processes and identify potential vulnerabilities. Black-box models resist both explanation and comprehensive security evaluation. The transparency-performance trade-off affects security.

Data quality determines both capability and vulnerability. High-quality, diverse training data improves model performance but also expands attack surfaces for data poisoning. Rigorous data validation increases security but may reduce dataset size and model capability. Data governance proves foundational to security.

Organizational Dependencies

Technical security requires organizational support. The most sophisticated defensive techniques fail without proper implementation, monitoring, and maintenance. Technical capability without organizational maturity produces fragile security.

Conversely, strong organizational processes cannot compensate for fundamental technical vulnerabilities. Well-documented policies don't prevent adversarial examples. Mature governance doesn't eliminate privacy risks. Technical and organizational security must advance together. Cultural factors enable or undermine both technical and organizational security. Organizations that value and understand security implement stronger technical controls and follow more robust processes. Organizations that view security as an obstacle rather than an enabler struggle regardless of technical or organizational investments.

Societal Context

Regulatory requirements shape organizational priorities and resource allocation. Compliance drives security investments even when pure risk analysis might suggest different priorities. Regulation provides both constraints and enablers for security work.

Public awareness and expectations create market pressure for security improvements. Organizations with poor security track records face customer backlash and competitive disadvantage. The social license to operate increasingly depends on the demonstration of responsible AI development and deployment.

Adversarial capabilities evolve with broader technological and geopolitical trends. Nation-state cyber capabilities, criminal innovation, and activist tactics all influence the threat landscape. AI security cannot be separated from broader security dynamics.

Core Principles Revisited

Throughout our exploration, several core principles emerged repeatedly. These principles transcend specific techniques or frameworks, providing enduring guidance regardless of technological change.

Security as a System Property

Security cannot be bolted onto AI systems after design. It must be embedded from inception through architecture, implementation, testing, deployment, and operation. Security by design remains essential despite adding complexity and cost to development processes.

This principle applies at every scale. Individual models need secure training procedures. Applications need secure integration patterns. Organizations need secure development practices. The ecosystem needs secure supply chains and infrastructure. Security at one level proves insufficient if other levels remain vulnerable.

Defense in Depth

No single defensive technique provides complete protection. Layered defenses that address different attack vectors and operate at different system levels create resilient security. When one defense fails, others provide backup protection.

Defense in depth applies across dimensions. Technical defenses combine with organizational processes and cultural factors. Preventive controls combine with detective and responsive capabilities. Design-time security combines with runtime monitoring. Comprehensive protection requires multiple complementary approaches.

Risk-Based Prioritization

Perfect security is simply impossible. Resources are finite. Trade-offs are inevitable. Effective security focuses effort where it matters most, based on risk assessment that considers threat likelihood and potential impact.

Risk-based approaches require an understanding of the specific context. High-stakes medical AI requires a different level of security than low-risk recommendation systems. Customer-facing applications face different threats than internal tools. Thoughtful risk analysis guides appropriate security investment.

Continuous Adaptation

The threat landscape evolves continuously. New attack techniques emerge. System capabilities expand. Deployment contexts change. Static security measures become obsolete. Effective security requires continuous monitoring, learning, and adaptation.

Adaptation happens at multiple timescales. Real-time monitoring detects attacks, enabling immediate response. Periodic reviews identify emerging threats requiring new defenses. Long-term strategic planning anticipates future challenges. All timescales matter for sustained security.

Transparency and Accountability

Security through obscurity fails against sophisticated adversaries. Transparent security approaches enable independent evaluation, encourage responsible disclosure, and build trust with stakeholders. Accountability mechanisms ensure security commitments translate into actual practices.

Transparency must be balanced with operational security. Publishing detailed vulnerability information before patches are available helps attackers. But the general principles, architectures, and approaches behind security should be open to scrutiny. Finding the right balance requires judgment.

Human-Centered Security

Security ultimately serves human values and protects human interests. Technical excellence without ethical grounding proves insufficient. Security measures that create unusable systems or concentrate power inappropriately fail despite technical soundness.

Human-centered security considers the impacts on all stakeholders, including end users, affected communities, developers, operators, and society. It prioritizes fairness, privacy, dignity, and autonomy alongside traditional security objectives. Technology serves humanity, not the other way around.

9.2 Critical Challenges Ahead

Technical Frontiers

Several technical challenges will demand sustained research and innovation over the coming years.

Provable Security

Current AI security relies heavily on empirical evaluation. We test models against known attacks and hope they resist unknown attacks. This approach is insufficient for high-stakes applications in which failures have severe consequences. The field needs progress toward provable security guarantees. Formal verification, certified defenses, and mathematical bounds on robustness all contribute. But current techniques remain limited in scope and scalability. Extending provable guarantees to practical systems represents a major research challenge.

Progress requires interdisciplinary collaboration between AI researchers, formal methods experts, and security specialists. It needs new mathematical frameworks that integrate probability theory, optimization, and logic. Breakthroughs may emerge from unexpected directions.

Adaptive Adversaries

Most security research assumes static attack techniques. Real adversaries adapt. They observe defenses and develop new attacks exploiting defensive blind spots. This adaptive dynamic creates an arms race where defenses quickly become obsolete.

We need security approaches that remain effective against adaptive adversaries. Techniques include randomization, creating uncertainty for attackers, moving-target defenses, dynamically changing attack surfaces, and adversarial training with continually updated attack methods. But fundamental questions remain about the limits of defense against intelligent adaptation.

Game-theoretic frameworks may provide insights into the dynamics between defenders and attackers. Understanding equilibrium strategies could guide robust defensive investments. But applying game theory to complex real-world systems with imperfect information presents significant challenges.

Scalable Evaluation

Comprehensive security evaluation requires testing against diverse attacks across multiple threat models. Evaluation costs scale with model size, number of potential attacks, and required statistical confidence. Current evaluation approaches don't scale to the largest models or most complex systems.

Automated evaluation techniques help, but remain limited. Adversarial example generation can be automated, but it doesn't cover all attack types. Privacy auditing tools exist, but don't capture all privacy risks. We need more comprehensive, automated, scalable evaluation frameworks.

Evaluation must also address dynamic systems that change through continual learning or human feedback. Static assessment of a model version provides limited assurance if the model updates frequently. Online evaluation during operation presents both technical and methodological challenges.

Multimodal and Generative Systems

Foundation models that process and generate multiple modalities pose novel security challenges. Cross-modal attacks exploit interactions between modalities. Generative capabilities enable new attack vectors, such as prompt injection and jailbreaking. Current security techniques developed for discriminative single-modality models require significant adaptation.

Securing generative systems proves particularly challenging because the output space is unbounded. Classifiers produce outputs from fixed sets. Generative models can produce novel, unexpected outputs. Ensuring harmful content is never generated requires different approaches than ensuring correct classification.

Aligning powerful generative models with human values poses both technical and philosophical challenges. How do we specify and enforce value alignment when values vary across individuals and cultures? Technical solutions require ethical foundations.

Organizational Imperatives

Technical advances alone won't secure AI systems. Organizational capabilities must keep pace.

Talent Development at Scale

AI security requires rare skill combinations of security expertise, AI knowledge, software engineering capability, and domain understanding. Current talent supply falls far short of demand. This gap will persist for years.

Accelerating talent development requires multiple approaches. Educational institutions must integrate AI security into curricula. Industry training programs must upskill existing professionals. Tools and frameworks must lower expertise requirements for common tasks. No single approach suffices.

Organizations cannot wait for perfect external talent. Develop internal capabilities through training, mentorship, and experience. Create career paths to retain developed talent. Build communities of practice where people learn from each other.

Sustainable Security Investment

Security requires sustained investment even when no incidents occur. This creates tension with short-term financial pressures. Organizations must justify security spending when benefits are invisible and costs are concrete.

Quantifying security value remains difficult. Traditional ROI calculations don't capture prevented incidents that would have occurred without security. Alternative metrics like reduced risk exposure, increased customer trust, and expanded market access help, but lack the precision of direct cost-benefit analysis.

Long-term thinking proves essential. Security underinvestment creates technical debt that becomes expensive to remediate later. Incident response costs far exceed prevention costs. But organizations with quarterly earnings pressure struggle with long-term investments. Leadership commitment becomes crucial.

Cross-Functional Integration

AI security cannot succeed as a siloed specialty. It requires integration across engineering, product, legal, compliance, and business functions. Breaking down organizational silos challenges existing structures and cultures.

Integration mechanisms include embedded security experts, cross-functional teams, integrated tools and workflows, and shared metrics and incentives. But mechanisms alone don't change culture. Sustained effort builds collaborative relationships and mutual understanding across functions.

Security must prove its value to other functions. Engineers need security that enables rather than blocks innovation. Product teams need security to expand market opportunities. Legal and compliance need security to reduce regulatory risk. Demonstrating value builds support for integration.

9.3 Reasons for Optimism

Despite formidable challenges, there are substantial reasons for optimism. Progress is happening across technical, organizational, and policy dimensions.

Technical Progress

AI security research advances rapidly. Academic publications on adversarial robustness, privacy preservation, fairness, and interpretability increase exponentially. Major conferences now feature dedicated tracks on trustworthy AI. The research community has mobilized.

Defensive techniques improve measurably. Adversarial training increases robustness substantially compared to standard training. Differential privacy enables useful model training with meaningful privacy guarantees. Certified defenses provide provable bounds for limited threat models. Progress continues despite remaining challenges.

Open source tools democratize security capabilities. Libraries for adversarial robustness testing, privacy accounting, bias detection, and interpretability enable smaller organizations to implement sophisticated techniques. Shared infrastructure accelerates field progress.

Organizational Maturation

Organizations increasingly recognize the importance of AI security and invest accordingly. Dedicated AI security teams emerge at major companies. Security becomes a standard consideration in development processes rather than an afterthought. Maturity advances across the industry.

Best practices are being codified and shared. Industry frameworks, implementation guides, and case studies accumulate. Organizations learn from each other's experiences. The field benefits from increasing transparency about what works and what doesn't.

Tools and platforms specifically designed for AI security reach the market. Automated testing tools, monitoring platforms, model governance systems, and security-aware development environments mature rapidly. Better tools enable better security at lower cost.

Policy Development

Governments and regulators take AI security challenges seriously. The EU AI Act establishes comprehensive requirements. U.S. agencies issue guidance and conduct enforcement. Asian countries develop their own frameworks. Regulatory attention drives organizational action.

Standards bodies produce increasingly detailed specifications. ISO standards, NIST frameworks, and industry-specific guidelines provide guidance on implementation. Standards enable consistent practices and simplify compliance.

International cooperation on AI governance advances despite geopolitical tensions. Shared recognition of AI risks motivates coordination. Forums for dialogue and information sharing emerge. While challenges remain, cooperation progresses.

Community Building

The AI security community continues to grow and strengthen. Conferences attract thousands of participants. Online forums facilitate knowledge sharing. Professional networks connect practitioners across organizations and countries. Community provides support and accelerates learning.

Collaborative projects produce shared resources benefiting everyone. Benchmark datasets enable objective comparison. Open source tools provide a common infrastructure. Shared threat intelligence improves collective defense. Cooperation complements competition.

Diversity within the community increases. More perspectives contribute to problem-solving. Representation from different backgrounds, geographies, and organizational types enriches the field. Diverse communities produce better security.

9.4 Your Role in the Future

Universal Responsibilities

Every person working with AI systems carries security responsibilities regardless of their formal role.

Awareness

Understand AI security fundamentals even if you're not a security specialist. Recognize common vulnerabilities. Know when to seek security expertise. Ask security questions during design and development. Awareness enables everyone to contribute to security.

Stay informed about evolving threats and defenses. Follow security news and research. Participate in training and awareness programs. Understanding changes as the field develops. Continuous learning maintains relevant awareness.

Advocacy

Speak up about security concerns. Question designs that sacrifice security unnecessarily. Advocate for adequate security resources. Support colleagues raising security issues. Security culture requires many voices, not just security teams.

Frame security in terms that matter to your audience. Executives respond to business risk and competitive advantage. Engineers respond to technical elegance and reduced technical debt. Find arguments that resonate while maintaining security substance.

Action

Implement security practices within your scope of control. Write secure code. Follow secure development processes. Report vulnerabilities. Respond to incidents. Action matters more than perfect understanding. Do what you can with what you know.

Hold yourself and others accountable. Deliver on security commitments. Call out security theater that creates an appearance without substance. Demand genuine security, not checkbox compliance. Accountability makes commitments real.

Role-Specific Contributions

Different roles enable different contributions to AI security.

Researchers and Academics

Advance fundamental understanding of AI security challenges and solutions. Explore techniques that may not have immediate practical application but expand the field's knowledge. Publish openly to share discoveries. Teach the next generation of practitioners.

Bridge the gap between research and practice. Collaborate with industry to understand real-world constraints. Evaluate techniques in realistic settings. Develop usable tools and frameworks that practitioners can adopt. Research matters most when it influences practice.

Consider broader implications of research directions. Some research might inadvertently strengthen attackers more than defenders. Other research might concentrate power inappropriately. Researchers carry responsibility for foreseeable impacts of their work.

Engineers and Developers

Implement security practices in development work. Threat model designs. Test for vulnerabilities. Harden code. Monitor production systems. Daily engineering decisions determine actual security outcomes.

Build security into systems from the start rather than retrofitting later. Early security considerations cost less and achieve better results. Push back against unrealistic schedules that sacrifice security. Advocate for technical approaches that enable rather than sacrifice security.

Share knowledge with other engineers. Document security patterns and anti-patterns. Conduct internal training. Review colleagues' code with security in mind. Engineering excellence includes security excellence.

Product and Business Leaders

Prioritize security in product strategy and resource allocation. Security investments compete with features and performance. Make informed trade-offs based on risk assessment. Sometimes security deserves priority over new capabilities.

Communicate security value to executives and stakeholders. Translate technical risks into business language. Quantify impacts where possible. Frame security as enabling business objectives rather than constraining them.

Build security into product success metrics. Measure security alongside traditional metrics like adoption, revenue, and user satisfaction. Metrics shape behavior. Including security in definitions of success changes priorities and outcomes.

Security Specialists

Provide expertise enabling others to build secure systems. Consult on designs. Review implementations. Conduct security assessments. Respond to incidents. Specialized expertise multiplies when shared effectively.

Make security accessible rather than arcane. Translate complex security concepts into practical guidance. Build tools that automate security tasks. Create resources that enable self-service. Reducing friction increases security adoption.

Maintain technical excellence while developing business acumen. Understand organizational dynamics and incentives. Recognize constraints others face. Propose solutions that work within real-world limitations while maintaining security substance.

Policy Makers and Regulators

Develop regulations that protect without unnecessarily constraining beneficial innovation. Risk-based approaches focus requirements where they matter most. Flexible frameworks accommodate technological change better than prescriptive rules.

Engage with technical communities to understand the practical implications of proposed rules. Well-intentioned regulations can have unintended consequences. Input from practitioners improves regulatory effectiveness.

Support research and development advancing AI security. Public funding for foundational research generates social returns exceeding private returns. Regulatory certainty enables long-term private investment. Policy shapes the environment in which security innovation occurs.

Educators and Trainers

Prepare the next generation of AI security practitioners. Integrate security into AI curricula. Teach security principles alongside technical skills.

Students who understand security fundamentals from the start build more secure systems throughout their careers.

Develop accessible educational resources for diverse audiences. Not everyone needs a PhD-level understanding. Different roles require different knowledge. Create learning paths tailored to diverse backgrounds and objectives.

Foster interdisciplinary thinking. AI security requires combining expertise from multiple fields. Encourage students to develop both depth and breadth. Build collaboration skills alongside technical capabilities.

9.5 A Vision for 2035

The Achievable Future

Ten years from now, what could AI security look like if we make the right choices and investments today?

Secure by Default

In 2035, secure development practices are standard rather than exceptional. Security tools integrate seamlessly into development workflows. Frameworks and platforms provide security by default, requiring deliberate action to reduce protection rather than deliberate action to add it.

Automated testing catches common vulnerabilities before deployment. Continuous monitoring detects attacks in production. Incident response procedures enable rapid containment and recovery. Security operates smoothly rather than creating friction.

Educational programs have produced generations of practitioners who understand the fundamentals of AI security. Security is not an afterthought but an integral part of AI engineering. Cultural change has embedded security into professional identity.

Mature Defenses

Defensive techniques have advanced substantially from where they are today. Adversarial training produces robust models by default. Privacy-preserving techniques enable valuable applications without compromising individual privacy. Certified defenses provide provable guarantees for critical applications.

Standardized security testing validates system security before deployment. Independent auditors verify security claims. Regulatory frameworks enforce minimum security standards. Poor security creates a competitive disadvantage rather than a competitive advantage.

Open source security infrastructure provides common foundations. Organizations build on shared tools and frameworks rather than reinventing solutions. Community-developed benchmarks enable objective security evaluation and comparison.

Trustworthy Ecosystem

Supply chains for AI systems are transparent and verifiable. Models, datasets, and frameworks carry attestations about provenance and security properties. Automated tools verify integrity throughout development and deployment.

Information sharing enables collective defense. Threat intelligence flows freely within appropriate trust boundaries. Organizations learn from each other's incidents without fear of reputational damage. Cooperation strengthens overall ecosystem security.

International regulatory frameworks are harmonized, reducing compliance complexity. Standards are mature and widely adopted. Best practices are codified and easily accessible. The ecosystem supports security rather than creating obstacles.

Ethical Integration

Security and ethics are deeply integrated rather than separate concerns. Systems are secure, fair, private, and accountable. Trade-offs between objectives are explicit and thoughtful rather than implicit and overlooked.

Diverse perspectives shape AI development, ensuring systems serve broad populations rather than narrow interests. Marginalized communities participate in design rather than simply being affected by outcomes. Power is distributed rather than concentrated.

Long-term thinking guides development decisions. Sustainability considerations include not just environmental impact but also social and security sustainability. Systems are designed for longevity and adaptability rather than obsolescence.

The Required Commitments

Achieving this vision requires commitments from all stakeholders.

Sustained Investment

Adequate funding for security research, development, and implementation. Resources for talent development. Investment in infrastructure and tools. Security requires money, and short-term thinking undermines long-term success.

Collaborative Culture

Breaking down silos within organizations and between organizations. Sharing knowledge and resources. Building trust, enabling cooperation. Competition on features and performance, but cooperation on security.

Regulatory Wisdom

Thoughtful regulation that protects without overreaching. Flexibility accommodating technological change. International coordination reduces fragmentation. Support for security innovation through funding and incentives.

Individual Responsibility

Every practitioner understands their security role and executes it well. Continuous learning as threats evolve. Speaking up about concerns. Acting with integrity and accountability.

Long-Term Thinking

Patience with the slow work of building enduring security. Resisting pressure for shortcuts. Investing in foundations even when payoffs are distant. Thinking about impacts beyond quarterly earnings or election cycles.

9.6 The Call to Action

What You Can Do This Week

Don't wait for perfect circumstances or complete understanding. Start now with concrete actions.

Assess your current security posture. Review systems you work on. Identify security gaps. Prioritize based on risk. Small improvements compound over time.

Learn something new about AI security. Read a paper. Watch a presentation. Experiment with a security tool. Continuous learning maintains relevant expertise.

Start a security conversation. Discuss security with colleagues. Raise concerns about systems you're developing. Ask questions in design reviews. Normalizing security discussions improves security culture.

Fix one vulnerability. Patch one security issue. Implement one defensive technique. Update one insecure practice. Tangible improvements matter more than perfect plans.

Share knowledge. Write about what you've learned. Present at team meetings. Answer questions on forums. Knowledge sharing multiplies your impact.

What You Can Do This Month

Build on immediate actions with sustained effort.

Conduct a threat modeling exercise. Pick one system and systematically analyze potential attacks against it. Document findings. Share with the team. Understanding threats guides better defenses.

Implement security testing. Add adversarial testing to your development pipeline. Set up bias detection. Configure privacy auditing. Automated testing catches issues early.

Start training others. Organize lunch-and-learn sessions. Create internal documentation. Mentor junior team members. Growing team capabilities increases overall security.

Engage with the community. Attend a meetup or conference. Join online forums. Follow researchers and practitioners. Community connection accelerates learning and provides support.

Advocate for resources. Make the business case for security investment. Propose specific projects with clear objectives. Demonstrate value through small wins. Resource advocacy enables larger improvements.

What You Can Do This Year

Strategic initiatives require longer time scales.

Build a comprehensive security program. Establish policies, processes, and tools. Assign responsibilities. Define metrics. Create sustainable security capabilities rather than ad hoc efforts.

Develop specialized expertise. Deep dive into specific security domains, such as adversarial robustness, privacy preservation, and fairness. Specialized expertise enables advanced contributions.

Contribute to the broader ecosystem. Publish research or implementation experiences. Contribute to open source tools. Participate in standards development. Individual contributions strengthen the field.

Influence organizational culture. Recognize good security practices. Celebrate security successes. Make security a valued part of engineering excellence. Culture change takes time but creates a lasting impact.

Build strategic partnerships. Connect with researchers, other practitioners, and organizations. Collaborative relationships enable knowledge sharing and joint problem solving.

9.7 The Final Word

This Moment Matters

We stand at a pivotal moment in the development of artificial intelligence. Decisions made now about security will shape outcomes for decades. Systems deployed today will operate in tomorrow's critical infrastructure. Practices established now will become tomorrow's standards or technical debt.

This moment demands the best from everyone working with AI systems. It requires technical excellence, organizational commitment, ethical grounding, and sustained effort. The challenges are real and substantial. The consequences of failure include not just security breaches but societal harms on an unprecedented scale.

Yet this moment also offers a tremendous opportunity. You have the chance to shape foundational security infrastructure. Your contributions ripple through the ecosystem, affecting colleagues, customers, and communities. The work you do today enables tomorrow's beneficial AI applications while preventing tomorrow's harms.

The Reality of Progress

Progress in AI security will not be linear or universal. Setbacks will occur. New vulnerabilities will emerge. Some organizations will excel while others lag. Perfect security will remain elusive.

But meaningful progress is achievable through sustained effort. Systems can be substantially more secure than they are today. Organizations can develop genuine security capabilities. The ecosystem can establish effective security foundations. Progress requires persistence rather than perfection.

Celebrate incremental improvements while maintaining ambitious goals. Each vulnerability fixed, each security practice adopted, each practitioner trained represents real progress. These individual improvements aggregate into field-level advancement.

The Journey Continues

This book concludes, but your AI security journey continues. The knowledge you've gained here provides a foundation, not a destination. The field evolves continuously, requiring continuous learning and adaptation.

Stay curious about new developments. Question assumptions, including those presented in this book. Experiment with new techniques. Learn from failures. Share discoveries with others. The journey rewards those who maintain intellectual humility and openness.

Build on what came before while innovating for what comes next. Respect the work that established current practices and knowledge. But don't be constrained by existing approaches. Novel challenges may require novel solutions.

Your Contribution Matters

You might wonder whether individual contributions matter when challenges are so large and systemic. They do. Security is built from countless individual decisions and actions. Every line of code written, every design reviewed, every vulnerability reported, every lesson shared contributes to collective security.

Your specific contribution is unique. Your perspective, experiences, skills, and position enable contributions others cannot make. The combination of everyone's unique contributions creates comprehensive security that no individual or organization can achieve on their own.

Don't wait for someone else to solve these problems. Don't assume your contribution is too small to matter. Act within your sphere of influence. Your actions, combined with others', create momentum toward more secure AI systems.

The Responsibility is Ours

No one else will secure AI systems if we don't. No magical solution will emerge without hard work. No authority will mandate security if we don't demonstrate its importance. The responsibility falls on everyone working with AI to ensure these powerful technologies serve humanity safely.

This responsibility is not a burden alone but an opportunity and a privilege. We get to shape how artificial intelligence develops and affects society. We influence whether AI amplifies human potential or amplifies human vulnerabilities. We determine whether AI concentrates power or distributes benefits.

Carrying this responsibility well requires the best of our technical abilities, ethical judgment, and collaborative spirit. It demands that we think beyond immediate deadlines to long-term consequences. It asks us to consider not just what we can build but what we should build and how to build it securely.

The Future Awaits

The future of AI security is not predetermined. It will be shaped by the choices and actions of people like you. Technical innovations, organizational practices, regulatory frameworks, and cultural norms will all emerge from human decisions.

Choose wisely. Act with integrity. Build with security and ethics integrated from the start. Collaborate generously. Think long-term. Hold yourself and others accountable. Contribute to the ecosystem. Mentor the next generation.

The systems you secure today will operate in a world you helped create. The practices you establish will guide others. The knowledge you share will inform decisions beyond your direct influence. Your legacy extends far beyond any single system or project.

Go forth with knowledge, purpose, and commitment. Build secure AI systems that deserve trust. Share your expertise with others. Learn continuously. Collaborate generously. Question assumptions. Think like adversaries. Design with users in mind. Consider societal impacts. Hold yourself and others accountable.

The stakes are immense. The challenges are real. The work is hard. But the opportunity to contribute to secure, beneficial AI systems that amplify human potential while protecting human values makes it all worthwhile.

Build wisely. Build securely. Build a future where artificial intelligence serves humanity.

The responsibility is ours. The moment is now. The future awaits your contribution.

Chapter Summary

This concluding chapter synthesized insights across all dimensions of AI security and issued a call to action for the future.

We explored how technical, organizational, and societal challenges interconnect, creating complex systems where actions in one area affect others. Core principles emerged, including security as a system property, defense-in-depth, risk-based prioritization, continuous adaptation, transparency and accountability, and human-centered security.

Critical technical challenges ahead include achieving provable security guarantees, defending against adaptive adversaries, scaling security evaluation, and securing multimodal generative systems. Organizational imperatives include talent development at scale, sustainable security investment, and cross-functional integration.

Despite formidable challenges, there are substantial reasons for optimism. Technical progress in defensive techniques continues. Organizations mature in security practices. Policy development advances. The community grows and strengthens through collaboration.

We presented a vision for 2035 where security is the default, defenses are mature, the ecosystem is trustworthy, and ethics are integrated. Achieving this vision requires sustained investment, collaborative culture, regulatory wisdom, individual responsibility, and long-term thinking.

Everyone working with AI carries security responsibilities from awareness through advocacy to action. Different roles enable different specific contributions, but all roles matter. Progress happens through countless individual decisions and actions combining into collective advancement.

The call to action provided concrete steps for this week, this month, and this year. Immediate actions include assessing current security posture, learning, starting conversations, fixing vulnerabilities, and sharing knowledge. Longer-term actions include building comprehensive programs, developing expertise, contributing to the ecosystem, influencing culture, and building partnerships.

Key Takeaways

1. AI security challenges interconnect across technical, organizational, and societal dimensions. Isolated solutions prove insufficient. Comprehensive approaches addressing multiple dimensions simultaneously achieve better outcomes.

2. Core security principles transcend specific techniques and remain valuable despite technological change. Understand principles deeply rather than memorizing specific practices.

3. Perfect security is impossible, but meaningful progress is achievable. Don't let the pursuit of perfection prevent incremental improvements. Small gains compound over time.

4. Everyone working with AI carries security responsibilities regardless of formal role. Security culture requires many voices, not just security specialists.

5. The field needs sustained investment in research, development, talent, and infrastructure. Short-term thinking undermines long-term security. Advocate for adequate resources.

6. Technical excellence must combine with ethical grounding. Security without ethics proves insufficient and potentially dangerous. Consider who benefits and who might be harmed by the systems you secure.

7. Collaboration accelerates progress more than competition. Share knowledge, contribute to common infrastructure, and build on others' work. The ecosystem benefits when everyone contributes.

8. Individual contributions matter tremendously in this young field. Your unique perspective and position enable contributions others cannot make. Don't wait for others to solve these problems.

9. Progress requires patience and persistence. Setbacks will occur. New vulnerabilities will emerge. Maintain commitment despite challenges and celebrate incremental improvements.

10. The future is not predetermined but will be shaped by choices made and actions taken now. Your decisions influence outcomes far beyond any single system. Build wisely and securely.

Reflection Questions

1. How has this book changed your understanding of AI security? What surprised you most? What challenged your assumptions? How will this knowledge influence your work?

2. What is your specific role in advancing AI security? What unique contributions can you make based on your position, skills, and context? What responsibilities do you carry?

3. What concrete actions will you take in the next week, month, and year to improve AI security? Be specific about commitments you're willing to make and follow through on.

4. How will you balance security with other priorities and constraints in your work? What trade-offs will you accept and what security fundamentals will you defend?

5. Who will you collaborate with to amplify your impact? What partnerships will you build within your organization and in the broader community?

6. How will you maintain ethical grounding as you work on AI security? What frameworks will guide your decisions when facing difficult trade-offs?

7. What knowledge gaps do you still have? What will you learn next to deepen your expertise? How will you structure ongoing learning as the field evolves?

8. How will you contribute to the broader AI security ecosystem? Will you share knowledge, contribute to open source, participate in standards development, or mentor others?

9. What is your personal vision for AI security in 2035? What role will you play in achieving that vision? What commitments are you willing to make?

10. Ten years from now, looking back on your AI security work, what will you be proudest of? What legacy do you want to leave?

Conclusion: Begin Now

You have finished this book, but your work in AI security has only begun. The knowledge you've gained provides a foundation for action. Understanding without implementation produces no security improvements.

The path forward is clear. Assess your current security posture honestly. Identify gaps between the current and desired states. Prioritize improvements based on risk. Make concrete commitments. Follow through with sustained effort.

Start small, but start now. You don't need perfect conditions or a complete understanding. Begin with awareness, advocacy, and action within your current sphere of influence. Small improvements compound over time into substantial progress.

Connect your individual efforts to the broader community. You are not alone in this work. Thousands of practitioners, researchers, policy makers, and educators share the commitment to secure AI systems. Collaborate, learn from others, and contribute your unique perspective.

Maintain realistic optimism. The challenges are real and will not be solved quickly or easily. Setbacks will occur. But meaningful progress is achievable through sustained effort. The vision of secure, beneficial AI systems serving humanity is worth pursuing.

Remember why this work matters. AI systems increasingly shape human lives in profound ways. Security enables beneficial applications while preventing harm. Your contribution to AI security directly impacts human wellbeing, dignity, and flourishing.

The responsibility is ours. The moment is now. The future awaits your contribution.

Build wisely. Build securely. Build a future worthy of the opportunity before us.

10

AI Governance Beyond Perimeter Security

Learning Objectives

By the end of this chapter, you will:

- Understand why traditional security paradigms fail to address AI-specific governance challenges.
- Identify and address the accountability vacuum in AI decision-making systems.
- Implement decision-sovereignty mapping to establish clear accountability structures.
- Distinguish between transparency theater and genuine intelligibility in AI systems.
- Establish adversarial thinking as a governance discipline within organizations.
- Design governance architectures that enable organizational control over AI behavior

- Build standing challenge functions with genuine authority to influence AI deployment.

Introduction: Beyond Castle Security

Most organizations approach AI governance like medieval castle builders. They construct towering walls of access controls, dig deep moats of network segmentation, and station guards at every API gateway they can find. Then they wonder why threats emerge from inside the walls. The uncomfortable truth about AI security is that we have inherited mental models from an era of static software and predictable attack vectors. AI systems do not behave like traditional software. They learn, adapt, and sometimes hallucinate their way into catastrophic decisions. Governing them requires abandoning the comfortable fiction that security means keeping bad actors out.

The real danger often lies in what your AI does when everything is working exactly as designed. Consider the fundamental disconnect in how most enterprises frame AI risk. Security teams obsess over data breaches, model theft, and adversarial attacks. These are legitimate concerns, but they represent perhaps twenty percent of the actual governance challenge. The other eighty percent lives in the mundane reality of AI systems making thousands of small decisions that compound into organizational blind spots, legal liabilities, and strategic misdirection.

When your customer service AI subtly discourages certain demographics from premium products, no firewall catches that. When your financial model learns to optimize for metrics that diverge from actual business health, no intrusion detection system raises an alarm. The breach is not in your perimeter. It is in your assumptions. This chapter establishes a governance framework that addresses these deeper challenges, moving beyond perimeter security to comprehensive organizational control over AI behavior.

We examine governance not as a compliance burden but as a strategic discipline ensuring that AI capabilities remain aligned with organizational interests. The framework presented here synthesizes insights from organizational theory, security engineering, and practical experience with deployed AI systems. Our goal is to provide actionable guidance for building governance structures that withstand the complexity of real-world AI deployment.

10.1 The Accountability Vacuum

The Fundamental Problem

Here is a thought experiment that should concern every executive. Ask your organization who is responsible when an AI system makes a decision that costs ten million dollars or destroys a critical customer relationship. Not who approved the system. Not who maintains it. Who is accountable for that specific decision at that specific moment?

In most organizations, this question produces either uncomfortable silence or a circular firing squad of finger-pointing. The data science team points to the business unit that requested the system. The business unit points to the IT team that deployed it. The IT team points to the vendor who provided the model. The vendor points to the data the organization provided for training. This accountability vacuum represents the single largest security vulnerability in enterprise AI, and almost no governance framework addresses it seriously.

We have created systems that make consequential decisions while existing in an organizational limbo where traditional chains of responsibility dissolve into algorithmic abstraction. When a human employee makes a bad decision, the accountability is very clear. Performance reviews, termination, and legal liability provide mechanisms for consequences when this occurs. However, when an AI system makes the same bad decision, accountability fragments across technical teams, business sponsors, and organizational leadership, often leaving no one genuinely responsible.

Sources of Accountability Failure

Several factors contribute to the accountability vacuum:

Technical Opacity makes it difficult to explain why AI systems reach specific conclusions. Even experts struggle to trace decision paths through complex neural networks. This opacity creates plausible deniability. No one can be held accountable for decisions no one can explain.

Distributed Development spreads responsibility across many contributors. Data collectors, feature engineers, model trainers, validators, deployers, and operators all contribute to system behavior. When failure occurs, each contributor can point to others whose work might have caused the problem.

Continuous Learning means systems change after deployment. The validated model may differ from the model used for making production decisions. Who is accountable for behavior that emerged through learning rather than explicit programming?

Vendor Dependencies introduce external parties into accountability chains. Organizations using third-party models or APIs depend on vendors whose internal decisions affect system behavior. Contracts rarely establish clear accountability for AI decision quality.

Organizational Silos separate technical and business accountability. Data science teams focus on model accuracy. Business teams focus on outcomes. Neither fully owns the relationship between model behavior and business impact.

Consequences of the Vacuum

The accountability vacuum creates several dangerous conditions:

Risk Blindness: When no one owns AI risk, no one monitors it comprehensively. Teams track the metrics they control while systemic risks accumulate unobserved.

Slow Response: Incidents require coordination across teams that rarely communicate with one another. By the time accountable parties are identified and coordinated, the damage has compounded.

Learning Failures: Without clear accountability, organizations fail to learn from AI failures. Problems recur because no one owns the improvement process.

Regulatory Exposure: Regulators increasingly expect clear accountability for algorithmic decisions. Organizations unable to demonstrate accountability face enforcement risk.

Strategic Drift: AI systems optimize for their training objectives, which may diverge from organizational strategy over time. Without accountability, this drift continues unchecked.

10.2 Decision Sovereignty Mapping

The Core Concept

Effective AI governance requires what we call decision sovereignty mapping. Every AI system should have clear documentation of which decisions it can make autonomously, which require human confirmation, and which it should never touch, regardless of confidence level. This framework borrows from military concepts of rules of engagement. A soldier with a weapon has clear boundaries about when and how force can be applied. Your AI systems deserve the same clarity.

This is not about limiting AI capability. It is about creating genuine accountability structures that survive contact with reality. Decision sovereignty mapping establishes explicit boundaries that enable both effective AI utilization and meaningful human oversight. The absence of such boundaries creates the accountability vacuum discussed above.

Decision Categories

Decision sovereignty mapping categorizes AI decisions into distinct zones with different governance requirements:

Full Autonomy Zone: Decisions the AI system can make without human involvement. These should be low-stakes, high-volume decisions where AI judgment is reliable and errors are easily correctable. Examples include routing customer service inquiries, basic content recommendations, and routine data processing.

Assisted Decision Zone: Decisions where AI provides recommendations that humans approve. The system generates options and assessments, but humans make final choices. Examples include hiring recommendations, credit decisions above certain thresholds, and medical diagnosis suggestions.

Human Primary Zone: Decisions where humans lead, and AI provides supporting information. AI contributes to data analysis and pattern recognition, but decision-making authority clearly rests with humans. Examples include strategic planning, major investments, and novel responses to situations.

Prohibited Zone: Decisions the AI system must never make, regardless of confidence. These involve ethical red lines, legal restrictions, or strategic considerations that require human judgment in all cases. Examples include decisions affecting fundamental rights, irreversible actions with major consequences, and situations involving protected classes.

Mapping Methodology

Creating effective decision sovereignty maps requires systematic analysis:

Decision Inventory: Catalog all decisions the AI system makes or influences. Include both explicit decisions, such as approvals and rejections, as well as implicit decisions, such as prioritization and filtering. Many AI systems make far more decisions than their creators initially recognize.

Impact Assessment: For each decision type, assess potential impacts. Consider financial magnitude, reversibility, affected parties, and downstream consequences. High-impact decisions warrant more restrictive sovereignty classification.

Confidence Evaluation: Assess how reliably the AI system makes each decision type. Consider historical accuracy, edge-case handling, and failure-mode characteristics. Unreliable decision types require more human involvement.

Context Sensitivity: Identify decisions whose appropriate sovereignty level varies with context. A decision that can be autonomous in normal conditions might require human oversight during unusual circumstances.

Escalation Triggers: Define conditions that trigger decisions to be escalated to higher oversight levels. Triggers might include confidence thresholds, unusual patterns, or specific input characteristics.

Implementation Architecture

Decision sovereignty requires technical implementation that enforces boundaries:

Decision Gates intercept AI outputs and route them according to sovereignty classifications. For autonomous decisions, gates pass outputs directly. For assisted decisions, gates queue outputs for human review. For prohibited decisions, gates block outputs and raise alerts.

Confidence Thresholds trigger escalation when AI certainty falls below defined levels. Low-confidence decisions automatically route to higher oversight levels regardless of decision type classification.

Audit Logging records all decisions with sufficient context for later review. Logs should capture the decision, the sovereignty level applied, any human involvement, and the outcome.

Override Mechanisms enable authorized humans to intervene at any level. Even autonomous decisions should include the capability to intervene in exceptional circumstances.

Feedback Loops connect decision outcomes to sovereignty classifications. Patterns of poor outcomes in autonomous zones should trigger reclassification to more restrictive levels.

10.3 From Transparency to Intelligibility

The Transparency Trap

The AI governance industry has developed an almost religious devotion to transparency. Publishing model cards, documenting training data, and disclosing algorithmic approaches have become standard practices. These activities create compliance artifacts and provide legal cover. However, transparency without intelligibility is theater. It satisfies procedural requirements while doing almost nothing for actual governance.

What matters is whether the humans who interact with and oversee AI systems can actually understand what those systems are doing and why. This is a harder problem than it sounds. Most organizations have exactly zero people who can genuinely explain why their production AI systems make specific decisions. They have people who can describe the training process. They have people who can read the output logs. They have people who can cite the accuracy metrics. But a genuine understanding of why a particular input produced a particular output remains elusive.

This gap between transparency and intelligibility creates false confidence. Organizations believe they understand their AI systems because they have documentation. They believe they can explain decisions because they have explainability tools. These beliefs crumble under scrutiny when actual decision explanations are needed for regulatory inquiries, legal proceedings, or incident response.

The Intelligibility Standard

Genuine intelligibility requires that relevant stakeholders can understand AI behavior at the level appropriate for their role:

Operators need to understand normal behavior patterns and recognize anomalies. They do not need to understand model internals, but they must recognize when systems behave unexpectedly.

Business Users need to understand how AI outputs relate to their decisions. They must grasp the limitations and appropriate use cases for AI recommendations.

Technical Teams need to understand model behavior sufficiently to diagnose problems, validate changes, and assess vulnerabilities. This requires a deeper understanding than mere documentation provides.

Leadership needs to understand AI capabilities and limitations sufficiently to make strategic decisions about deployment and risk acceptance.

Affected Parties need a sufficient understanding to exercise their rights. When AI decisions affect individuals, they should understand enough to evaluate fairness and pursue appeals.

Building Organizational Intelligibility

Real security through intelligibility means building organizational muscle for AI interpretation. This goes beyond hiring data scientists. Several practices contribute to organizational intelligibility:

Shared Vocabularies: Develop a common language between technical and business teams. Technical jargon excludes business stakeholders from governance. Business abstractions hide important technical nuances. Shared vocabulary enables genuine communication about AI behavior.

Escalation Pathways: Create clear procedures for raising concerns about AI behavior, even when metrics look normal. Humans often notice problems that quantitative monitoring misses. Effective escalation pathways capture this human judgment.

Interpretive Documentation: Invest in documentation that actually helps humans reason about machine decisions. This means going beyond architecture diagrams and API specifications to provide behavioral models, failure case examples, and narratives of decision logic.

Training Programs: Develop training that builds genuine understanding rather than procedural compliance. Effective training enables personnel to reason about AI behavior rather than just follow checklists.

Regular Explanability Exercises: Periodically require teams to explain specific AI decisions in detail. These exercises reveal gaps in understanding and motivate improvement. The inability to explain decisions indicates governance failure.

Technical Support for Intelligibility

Technology can support but not replace organizational intelligibility:

Explanation Generation: Tools like LIME and SHAP provide feature-level explanations for individual predictions. These tools support intelligibility when humans can interpret their outputs meaningfully.

Decision Tracing: Systems that record decision paths enable after-the-fact reconstruction of how specific outputs were produced. Tracing supports incident investigation and continuous learning.

Counterfactual Analysis: Tools that show how different inputs would produce different outputs help humans build mental models of AI behavior. Understanding how decisions change with inputs deepens understanding.

Behavioral Dashboards: Visualizations of AI behavior patterns over time help humans recognize normal operation and identify anomalies. Dashboards bridge raw data and human understanding.

However, tools alone do not create intelligibility. Organizations must invest in the human capabilities to use these tools effectively. The most sophisticated explanation tools provide no governance value if no one understands their outputs.

10.4 Adversarial Thinking as Governance Discipline

Beyond Traditional Red Teaming

Security professionals understand red teaming as a practice of simulating adversarial attacks. AI governance requires a more expansive version of this discipline. Traditional red teaming asks how attackers might compromise systems. AI governance red teaming asks a different question: how could this system produce terrible outcomes while functioning correctly?

This distinction matters profoundly. Traditional security assumes that bad outcomes require something going wrong, whether an attack, a bug, or a configuration error. AI systems can produce bad outcomes when everything works as designed. The threat model is not malicious actors. The threat model is reality, being more complex than the training data.

Consider an AI system that performs exactly as validated on test data but fails in production. This is not a bug. This is the fundamental nature of machine learning when encountering a distribution shift. Traditional security thinking struggles with failures that are not defects but rather inherent limitations of the approach. Adversarial governance thinking embraces this reality.

The Challenge Function

Organizations that take AI governance seriously should create standing challenge functions with real authority. These are not auditors who check boxes after deployment. They are internal skeptics empowered to delay or modify AI initiatives based on governance concerns.

The challenge function operates differently from traditional quality assurance. QA validates that systems meet specifications. The challenge function questions whether specifications adequately address potential harms. QA assumes that passing tests indicates readiness. The challenge function asks what scenarios tests might miss.

Effective challenge functions require several characteristics:

Independence: Challenge teams must report outside the development organization. Reporting to project sponsors creates conflicts that undermine skeptical assessment.

Authority: Challenge teams must have genuine power to delay or modify deployments. Advisory-only functions become bureaucratic speed bumps rather than governance mechanisms.

Expertise: Challenge teams need sufficient technical understanding to assess AI systems credibly. Non-technical challenge functions cannot meaningfully evaluate technical risks.

Resources: Challenge teams need time and tools for thorough assessment. Under-resourced challenge functions provide superficial review that creates false confidence.

Protection: Challenge team members need protection from retaliation for raising concerns. Governance requires the ability to deliver unwelcome news without career consequences.

Institutionalizing Skepticism

Beyond formal challenge functions, effective governance institutionalizes skepticism throughout the organization:

Pre-Mortem Analysis: Before deploying AI systems, conduct sessions to imagine future failures. Work backward from imagined disasters to identify potential causes. Pre-mortems surface risks that optimistic planning overlooks.

Devil's Advocate Roles: In decision meetings about AI deployment, explicitly assign someone to argue against deployment. Structured opposition ensures that concerns receive consideration.

Assumption Auditing: Regularly review the assumptions underlying AI systems. Training data assumptions, feature engineering assumptions, and deployment context assumptions all merit scrutiny. Assumption failure often precedes system failure.

Failure Mode Analysis: Systematically analyze how AI systems could fail and what consequences would follow. Prioritize failure modes by likelihood and impact. Design mitigations for high-priority failure modes.

External Perspective: Periodically engage external reviewers who lack organizational context. Fresh eyes identify issues that internal teams overlook due to familiarity.

The Friction Principle

Yes, adversarial thinking creates friction. Yes, challenge functions slow things down. That friction is the point. The speed advantage that AI provides is only valuable if you maintain control of the direction. Moving fast toward a cliff is not a competitive advantage.

Organizations must resist the temptation to optimize away governance friction. Every governance checkpoint removed enables a potential failure mode. The organizations that thrive are those that recognize AI governance not as a compliance burden but as a strategic discipline ensuring their technological capabilities remain aligned with their actual interests.

This does not mean maximizing friction. Effective governance finds the right level of scrutiny for different risk levels. Low-risk AI applications warrant lighter governance. High-risk applications warrant extensive review. The goal is calibrated friction that matches governance intensity to risk exposure.

10.5 Governance Architecture

Structural Components

Effective AI governance requires structural components integrated into organizational design:

AI Governance Board: A cross-functional body with authority over AI policy and major deployment decisions. The board should include representation from technical, legal, business, and ethics perspectives. It should have genuine authority rather than advisory status.

AI Risk Function: Dedicated resources for identifying, assessing, and monitoring AI risks. This function should report to enterprise risk management with dotted-line relationships to AI development teams.

AI Ethics Committee: A body focused specifically on the ethical implications of AI systems. The committee should include perspectives from affected communities, not just internal stakeholders.

Technical Governance Team: Engineers and data scientists focused on implementing governance controls, maintaining governance infrastructure, and providing technical guidance on governance questions.

Incident Response Team: A cross-functional team prepared to respond to AI incidents. This team should have pre-established procedures, communication channels, and decision authorities.

Process Framework

Governance structures require processes that translate policies into action:

Impact Assessment Process: Systematic evaluation of potential impacts before AI deployment. Assessments should cover the implications for accuracy, fairness, privacy, security, and broader societal effects.

Approval Workflow: Clear procedures for approving AI deployments based on risk classification. High-risk systems should require board-level approval. Lower-risk systems may have delegated approval authority.

Monitoring Protocol: Ongoing oversight of deployed AI systems. Monitoring should track performance, fairness, security indicators, and alignment with approved use cases.

Change Management: Procedures for modifying deployed AI systems. Changes above certain thresholds should require governance review similar to initial deployment.

Sunset Process: Procedures for retiring AI systems when they no longer serve organizational needs or when risks exceed benefits. Many organizations lack clear processes for ending AI deployments.

Policy Framework

Governance requires clear policies establishing expectations and requirements:

Acceptable Use Policy: Defines permitted and prohibited uses of AI within the organization. Should address both the development of new AI systems and the use of third-party AI services.

Data Governance Policy: Establishes requirements for data used in AI training and operation. Should address data quality, provenance, privacy, and retention.

Model Management Policy: Defines requirements for model development, validation, deployment, and monitoring. Should establish standards for documentation, testing, and version control.

Third-Party AI Policy: Establishes requirements for evaluating and using AI systems from external providers. Should address due diligence, contractual requirements, and ongoing monitoring.

Incident Response Policy: Defines procedures for responding to AI-related incidents. Should establish severity classifications, escalation procedures, and communication requirements.

Metrics and Accountability

Governance requires metrics that enable accountability:

Compliance Metrics: Track adherence to governance policies and procedures. Measure completion of required assessments, approval workflows, and monitoring activities.

Risk Metrics: Monitor AI risk exposure across the organization. Track risk levels by system, by use case, and in aggregate. Trend analysis reveals whether risk is increasing or decreasing.

Performance Metrics: Track AI system performance against governance-relevant criteria, including accuracy, fairness, and alignment with intended use cases.

Incident Metrics: Monitor AI-related incidents by frequency, severity, and root cause. Incident patterns reveal governance weaknesses requiring attention.

Process Metrics: Track the efficiency of the governance process. Measure time to approval, assessment quality, and stakeholder satisfaction. Governance should be effective without being unnecessarily burdensome.

10.6 Implementation Strategies

Maturity-Based Approach

Organizations at different governance maturity levels require different implementation strategies:

Foundational Stage: Organizations just beginning AI governance should focus on basic inventory and risk assessment. Know what AI systems you have. Understand their major risk factors. Establish basic policies. Build awareness among stakeholders.

Developing Stage: Organizations with basic governance in place should focus on process maturation. Implement systematic impact assessments. Establish formal approval workflows. Create monitoring capabilities. Build governance expertise.

Advanced Stage: Organizations with mature governance should focus on optimization and continuous improvement. Refine risk models based on experience. Streamline processes for efficiency. Develop predictive capabilities. Lead industry best practices.

Each stage builds on the previous. Attempting advanced governance without foundational capabilities creates complexity without benefit. However, organizations should not remain at lower maturity levels when their AI deployment warrants advancement.

Change Management

Implementing AI governance requires effective organizational change management:

Executive Sponsorship: Governance initiatives require visible support from organizational leadership. Without executive sponsorship, governance becomes a compliance exercise that teams work around rather than embrace.

Stakeholder Engagement: Involve affected stakeholders in governance design. Governance imposed from above generates resistance. Governance developed collaboratively generates ownership.

Impact Analysis: Conduct structured impact analyses to understand how governance changes affect roles, workflows, decision rights, and accountability. Clear visibility into impacts enables targeted communications, training, and adoption strategies, reducing resistance and unintended consequences.

Incremental Implementation: Implement governance incrementally rather than attempting comprehensive deployment at once. Start with the highest-risk systems. Learn from experience. Expand based on lessons learned.

Communication: Communicate governance rationale clearly. People are more likely to comply when they understand why governance matters. Explain the risks that governance addresses and the benefits it provides.

Training: Provide training that builds both skills and understanding. Technical training enables governance implementation. Conceptual training builds appreciation for governance value.

Common Implementation Challenges

Several challenges commonly impede governance implementation:

Speed Pressure: Business pressure to deploy AI quickly conflicts with thorough governance. Address this by demonstrating that governance catches problems cheaper than post-deployment remediation.

Expertise Gaps: Organizations often lack personnel with combined AI and governance expertise. Address this through targeted hiring, training, and external partnerships.

Tool Limitations: Governance tools remain immature compared to AI development tools. Address this by building custom capabilities where commercial tools fall short.

Organizational Resistance: Teams may resist governance as bureaucratic overhead. Address this by involving teams in governance design and demonstrating value through preventing problems.

Scope Ambiguity: Unclear boundaries around what constitutes AI complicate governance scope. Address this by establishing clear definitions and classification criteria.

10.7 Case Studies in AI Governance

Case Study 1: The Autonomous Credit Decision

A major financial institution deployed an AI system for credit decisions, granting full autonomy for decisions below a certain dollar threshold. The system performed excellently on accuracy metrics. However, governance review revealed that the system had developed a pattern of subtly disadvantaging applicants from certain geographic regions, a pattern that correlated with protected characteristics.

Root Cause: The decision-sovereignty mapping was based solely on dollar thresholds, without accounting for decision-pattern effects. No governance mechanism is in place to monitor for systematic bias in autonomous decisions.

Remediation: The institution implemented pattern monitoring across autonomous decisions, establishing fairness metrics with automatic escalation when thresholds were exceeded. Decision sovereignty mapping was revised to include pattern effects, not just individual decision impacts.

Lessons: Decision sovereignty cannot be based solely on the magnitude of individual decisions. Patterns across many small decisions can cause greater harm than individual large decisions. Governance must monitor decision patterns, not just individual decisions.

Case Study 2: The Transparency Theater

A healthcare organization published extensive documentation of its diagnostic AI system, including model cards, descriptions of training data, and algorithmic explanations. When a patient challenged a diagnosis, the organization discovered that no one could actually explain why the system had reached its specific conclusion. The documentation described the system in general terms but provided no capability for specific decision explanation.

Root Cause: The organization had conflated transparency artifacts with genuine intelligibility. The documentation described what the system was, but did not explain how it worked in specific cases.

Remediation: The organization invested in decision-level explainability tools and trained clinical staff in their use. They established requirements that any AI diagnosis must be accompanied by a human-understandable explanation.

Lessons: Transparency artifacts do not equal intelligibility. Organizations must be able to explain specific decisions, not just general system behavior. Governance should test explanation capability, not just documentation existence.

Case Study 3: The Missing Challenge Function

A technology company deployed an AI-powered content moderation system that performed well in testing. Within weeks of deployment, the system began incorrectly flagging content from specific cultural communities at dramatically higher rates. Internal teams had identified this risk before deployment, but lacked the authority to delay launch.

Root Cause: The organization had advisory governance but no challenge function with actual authority. Teams could raise concerns, but could not stop deployments they believed were premature.

Remediation: The organization established an AI ethics board with genuine authority to delay deployments. They created formal escalation procedures for pre-deployment concerns. They implemented a requirement for ethics board sign-off for high-risk deployments.

Lessons: Advisory governance is insufficient. Organizations need challenge functions with real authority. The ability to identify problems is worthless without the ability to act on that identification.

Case Study 4: The Accountability Gap

An insurance company faced a lawsuit over AI-driven claim denials. During discovery, it became clear that no one in the organization could identify who was responsible for the AI's decision criteria. The data science team had built the model. The business team had provided requirements. The IT team had deployed it. The claims team used it. No one owned it.

Root Cause: The organization had deployed AI without establishing clear accountability chains. Responsibility is fragmented across teams, with no single team owning the entire system.

Remediation: The organization established explicit ownership for all AI systems. Each system now has a designated accountable executive with clear responsibility for system behavior. Documentation requirements include accountability chain specification.

Lessons: Accountability must be explicit and documented. The accountability vacuum creates legal exposure and impedes effective governance. Every AI system needs a clearly identified responsible party.

Chapter Summary

This chapter established a comprehensive framework for AI governance that moves beyond traditional security paradigms:

The Accountability Vacuum: Most organizations cannot identify who is responsible for specific AI decisions. This accountability vacuum represents a critical governance failure. Sources include technical opacity, distributed development, continuous learning, vendor dependencies, and organizational silos.

Decision Sovereignty Mapping: Effective governance requires explicit documentation of AI decision authority. Systems should be clearly categorized into full autonomy, assisted decision, human primary, and prohibited zones. Implementation requires decision gates, confidence thresholds, and override mechanisms.

From Transparency to Intelligibility: Transparency artifacts like model cards create compliance theater without enabling genuine understanding. Intelligibility requires that relevant stakeholders can actually understand AI behavior at levels appropriate for their roles. Organizations must invest in shared vocabularies, escalation pathways, and interpretive documentation.

Adversarial Thinking: AI governance requires questioning how systems could produce terrible outcomes while functioning correctly. Organizations need standing challenge functions with genuine authority. Institutionalized skepticism through pre-mortems, devil's advocacy, and assumption auditing strengthens governance.

Governance Architecture: Effective governance requires structural components, including governance boards, risk functions, ethics committees, and incident response teams. Processes must translate policies into action through impact assessments, approval workflows, and monitoring protocols.

Implementation Strategies: Governance implementation should match organizational maturity. Change management requires executive sponsorship, stakeholder engagement, and incremental implementation. Common challenges include speed pressure, expertise gaps, and organizational resistance.

Key Takeaways

1. Traditional perimeter security models fail for AI systems. The real governance challenge is controlling what AI does when functioning correctly, not just defending against attacks.

2. The accountability vacuum represents the single largest governance vulnerability in enterprise AI. Every AI system needs clearly identified responsible parties for specific decisions.

3. Decision sovereignty mapping creates accountability by explicitly categorizing which decisions AI can make autonomously, which require human confirmation, and which are prohibited.

4. Transparency without intelligibility is theater. Organizations must invest in genuine understanding, not just documentation artifacts.

5. Adversarial thinking, as a governance discipline, asks how systems can fail even when working correctly. This requires standing challenge functions with real authority.

6. Governance friction is a feature, not a bug. Speed without direction is not a competitive advantage. Calibrated friction matches scrutiny to risk.

7. Governance architecture requires structural components, defined processes, and clear policies. Advisory-only functions are insufficient for effective governance.

8. Implementation should match organizational maturity. Attempting advanced governance without foundational capabilities creates complexity without benefit.

9. Case studies demonstrate that governance failures create legal exposure, reputational damage, and harm to affected parties. Proactive governance is far less costly than reactive remediation.

10. Effective AI governance is not a compliance burden but a strategic discipline ensuring AI capabilities remain aligned with organizational interests.

Reflection Questions

1. For an AI system in your organization, can you identify who is accountable for a specific decision made yesterday? What does your answer reveal about accountability structures?

2. Consider your organization's AI documentation. Does it enable genuine understanding of system behavior, or does it primarily satisfy compliance requirements? How would you know the difference?

3. If someone in your organization identified a serious concern about an AI deployment before launch, could they stop the deployment? What structural changes would enable this capability?

4. How would you create a decision sovereignty map for an AI system you work with? What decisions would fall into each category, and how would you justify those classifications?

5. What scenarios could cause your AI systems to produce terrible outcomes while functioning exactly as designed? How would your governance framework detect and respond to such scenarios?

6. Compare the governance friction in your organization for AI deployment versus traditional software deployment. Is the difference appropriate given the different risk profiles?

7. What would a standing challenge function look like in your organization? What authority would it need, and what organizational resistance would it face?

References

Standards and Frameworks

ISO/IEC 23894:2023. Information Technology — Artificial Intelligence — Guidance on Risk Management. International Organization for Standardization.

ISO/IEC 5338:2023. Information Technology — AI System Life Cycle Processes. International Organization for Standardization.

ISO/IEC 27001. Information Security Management Systems — Requirements. International Organization for Standardization.

ISO 26262. Road Vehicles — Functional Safety. International Organization for Standardization.

ISO/SAE 21434:2021. Road Vehicles — Cybersecurity Engineering. International Organization for Standardization / SAE International.

National Institute of Standards and Technology (NIST). AI Risk Management Framework (AI RMF 1.0). NIST AI 100-1, January 2023.

National Institute of Standards and Technology (NIST). Cybersecurity Framework (CSF). NIST, 2018 (updated 2024).

National Institute of Standards and Technology (NIST). Post-Quantum Cryptography Standardization Process. NIST, 2016–present.

OWASP (Open Web Application Security Project). OWASP Top 10 for Machine Learning Security. OWASP Foundation.

MITRE. ATLAS (Adversarial Threat Landscape for Artificial-Intelligence Systems). The MITRE Corporation.

MITRE. ATT&CK Framework. The MITRE Corporation.

IEEE. Ethically Aligned Design: A Vision for Prioritizing Human Well-Being with Autonomous and Intelligent Systems. IEEE Global Initiative on Ethics of Autonomous and Intelligent Systems.

Regulations and Legal Frameworks

European Parliament and Council. Regulation (EU) 2024/1689 Laying Down Harmonised Rules on Artificial Intelligence (EU AI Act). Official Journal of the European Union, 2024.

European Parliament and Council. Regulation (EU) 2016/679 on the Protection of Natural Persons with Regard to the Processing of Personal Data (General Data Protection Regulation / GDPR). Official Journal of the European Union, 2016.

U.S. Congress. Health Insurance Portability and Accountability Act (HIPAA). Public Law 104-191, 1996.

U.S. Food and Drug Administration (FDA). Artificial Intelligence and Machine Learning (AI/ML)-Enabled Medical Devices. FDA Guidance Documents.

U.S. Food and Drug Administration (FDA). Predetermined Change Control Plans for Machine Learning-Enabled Device Software Functions. FDA Draft Guidance, 2023.

California Consumer Privacy Act (CCPA). California Civil Code §1798.100 et seq., 2018.

U.S. Department of Labor. Occupational Safety and Health Administration (OSHA) Standards. 29 CFR Parts 1900–1999.

Adversarial Machine Learning

Goodfellow, I. J., Shlens, J., & Szegedy, C. (2015). Explaining and Harnessing Adversarial Examples. Proceedings of the International Conference on Learning Representations (ICLR).

Madry, A., Makelov, A., Schmidt, L., Tsipras, D., & Vladu, A. (2018). Towards Deep Learning Models Resistant to Adversarial Attacks. Proceedings of the International Conference on Learning Representations (ICLR).

Carlini, N., & Wagner, D. (2017). Towards Evaluating the Robustness of Neural Networks. Proceedings of the IEEE Symposium on Security and Privacy (S&P).

Szegedy, C., Zaremba, W., Sutskever, I., Bruna, J., Erhan, D., Goodfellow, I., & Fergus, R. (2014). Intriguing Properties of Neural Networks. Proceedings of the International Conference on Learning Representations (ICLR).

Kurakin, A., Goodfellow, I., & Bengio, S. (2017). Adversarial Examples in the Physical World. Proceedings of the International Conference on Learning Representations (ICLR) Workshop.

Eykholt, K., Evtimov, I., Fernandes, E., Li, B., Rahmati, A., Xiao, C., Prakash, A., Kohno, T., & Song, D. (2018). Robust Physical-World Attacks on Deep Learning Visual Classification. Proceedings of the IEEE/CVF Conference on Computer Vision and Pattern Recognition (CVPR).

Data Poisoning and Backdoor Attacks

Biggio, B., Nelson, B., & Laskov, P. (2012). Poisoning Attacks Against Support Vector Machines. Proceedings of the International Conference on Machine Learning (ICML).

Gu, T., Dolan-Gavitt, B., & Garg, S. (2017). BadNets: Identifying Vulnerabilities in the Machine Learning Model Supply Chain. arXiv preprint arXiv:1708.06733.

Shafahi, A., Huang, W. R., Najibi, M., Suciu, O., Studer, C., Dumitras, T., & Goldstein, T. (2018). Poison Frogs! Targeted Clean-Label Poisoning Attacks on Neural Networks. Advances in Neural Information Processing Systems (NeurIPS).

Chen, X., Liu, C., Li, B., Lu, K., & Song, D. (2017). Targeted Backdoor Attacks on Deep Learning Systems Using Data Poisoning. arXiv preprint arXiv:1712.05526.

Privacy Attacks and Defenses

Shokri, R., Stronati, M., Song, C., & Shmatikov, V. (2017). Membership Inference Attacks Against Machine Learning Models. Proceedings of the IEEE Symposium on Security and Privacy (S&P).

Fredrikson, M., Jha, S., & Ristenpart, T. (2015). Model Inversion Attacks that Exploit Confidence Information and Basic Countermeasures. Proceedings of the ACM Conference on Computer and Communications Security (CCS).

Carlini, N., Tramer, F., Wallace, E., Jagielski, M., Herbert-Voss, A., Lee, K., Roberts, A., Brown, T., Song, D., Erlingsson, U., Oprea, A., & Raffel, C. (2021). Extracting Training Data from Large Language Models. Proceedings of the USENIX Security Symposium.

Dwork, C. (2006). Differential Privacy. Proceedings of the International Colloquium on Automata, Languages, and Programming (ICALP).

Abadi, M., Chu, A., Goodfellow, I., McMahan, H. B., Mironov, I., Talwar, K., & Zhang, L. (2016). Deep Learning with Differential Privacy. Proceedings of the ACM Conference on Computer and Communications Security (CCS).

Model Extraction

Tramèr, F., Zhang, F., Juels, A., Reiter, M. K., & Ristenpart, T. (2016). Stealing Machine Learning Models via Prediction APIs. Proceedings of the USENIX Security Symposium.

Orekondy, T., Schiele, B., & Fritz, M. (2019). Knockoff Nets: Stealing Functionality of Black-Box Models. Proceedings of the IEEE/CVF Conference on Computer Vision and Pattern Recognition (CVPR).

Federated Learning

McMahan, B., Moore, E., Ramage, D., Hampson, S., & y Arcas, B. A. (2017). Communication-Efficient Learning of Deep Networks from Decentralized Data. Proceedings of the International Conference on Artificial Intelligence and Statistics (AISTATS).

Kairouz, P., McMahan, H. B., et al. (2021). Advances and Open Problems in Federated Learning. Foundations and Trends in Machine Learning, 14(1–2), 1–210.

Bagdasaryan, E., Veit, A., Hua, Y., Estrin, D., & Shmatikov, V. (2020). How to Back Door Federated Learning. Proceedings of the International Conference on Artificial Intelligence and Statistics (AISTATS).

Explainability and Interpretability

Ribeiro, M. T., Singh, S., & Guestrin, C. (2016). "Why Should I Trust You?": Explaining the Predictions of Any Classifier (LIME). Proceedings of the ACM SIGKDD International Conference on Knowledge Discovery and Data Mining.

Lundberg, S. M., & Lee, S.-I. (2017). A Unified Approach to Interpreting Model Predictions (SHAP). Advances in Neural Information Processing Systems (NeurIPS).

Mitchell, M., Wu, S., Zaldivar, A., Barnes, P., Vasserman, L., Hutchinson, B., Spitzer, E., Raji, I. D., & Gebru, T. (2019). Model Cards for Model Reporting. Proceedings of the ACM Conference on Fairness, Accountability, and Transparency (FAccT).

Gebru, T., Morgenstern, J., Vecchione, B., Vaughan, J. W., Wallach, H., Daumé III, H., & Crawford, K. (2021). Datasheets for Datasets. Communications of the ACM, 64(12), 86–92.

Fairness in Machine Learning

Barocas, S., Hardt, M., & Narayanan, A. (2023). Fairness and Machine Learning: Limitations and Opportunities. MIT Press.

Buolamwini, J., & Gebru, T. (2018). Gender Shades: Intersectional Accuracy Disparities in Commercial Gender Classification. Proceedings of the ACM Conference on Fairness, Accountability, and Transparency (FAccT).

Chouldechova, A. (2017). Fair Prediction with Disparate Impact: A Study of Bias in Recidivism Prediction Instruments. Big Data, 5(2), 153–163.

Kleinberg, J., Mullainathan, S., & Raghavan, M. (2017). Inherent Trade-Offs in the Fair Determination of Risk Scores. Proceedings of Innovations in Theoretical Computer Science (ITCS).

Cryptography and Quantum Computing

Shor, P. W. (1994). Algorithms for Quantum Computation: Discrete Logarithms and Factoring. Proceedings of the Annual Symposium on Foundations of Computer Science (FOCS).

Grover, L. K. (1996). A Fast Quantum Mechanical Algorithm for Database Search. Proceedings of the Annual ACM Symposium on Theory of Computing (STOC).

Avanzi, R., et al. CRYSTALS-Kyber: Algorithm Specifications and Supporting Documentation. NIST Post-Quantum Cryptography Standardization, Round 3 Submission.

Bernstein, D. J., et al. SPHINCS+: Submission to the NIST Post-Quantum Project. NIST Post-Quantum Cryptography Standardization.

Bernstein, D. J., Buchmann, J., & Ding, J. (Eds.). (2009). Post-Quantum Cryptography. Springer.

Gentry, C. (2009). Fully Homomorphic Encryption Using Ideal Lattices. Proceedings of the Annual ACM Symposium on Theory of Computing (STOC).

Neural Network Architectures

Vaswani, A., Shazeer, N., Parmar, N., Uszkoreit, J., Jones, L., Gomez, A. N., Kaiser, Ł., & Polosukhin, I. (2017). Attention Is All You Need. Advances in Neural Information Processing Systems (NeurIPS).

Devlin, J., Chang, M.-W., Lee, K., & Toutanova, K. (2019). BERT: Pre-training of Deep Bidirectional Transformers for Language Understanding. Proceedings of the Conference of the North American Chapter of the Association for Computational Linguistics (NAACL).

Brown, T. B., Mann, B., Ryder, N., et al. (2020). Language Models are Few-Shot Learners (GPT-3). Advances in Neural Information Processing Systems (NeurIPS).

Hochreiter, S., & Schmidhuber, J. (1997). Long Short-Term Memory. Neural Computation, 9(8), 1735–1780.

Cho, K., van Merrienboer, B., Gulcehre, C., Bahdanau, D., Bougares, F., Schwenk, H., & Bengio, Y. (2014). Learning Phrase Representations Using RNN Encoder-Decoder for Statistical Machine Translation (GRU). Proceedings of the Conference on Empirical Methods in Natural Language Processing (EMNLP).

Kipf, T. N., & Welling, M. (2017). Semi-Supervised Classification with Graph Convolutional Networks. Proceedings of the International Conference on Learning Representations (ICLR).

Robust and Certified Defenses

Cohen, J., Rosenfeld, E., & Kolter, J. Z. (2019). Certified Adversarial Robustness via Randomized Smoothing. Proceedings of the International Conference on Machine Learning (ICML).

Wong, E., & Kolter, J. Z. (2018). Provable Defenses Against Adversarial Examples via the Convex Outer Adversarial Polytope. Proceedings of the International Conference on Machine Learning (ICML).

Papernot, N., McDaniel, P., Wu, X., Jha, S., & Swami, A. (2016). Distillation as a Defense to Adversarial Perturbations Against Deep Neural Networks. Proceedings of the IEEE Symposium on Security and Privacy (S&P).

Datasets and Benchmarks

Deng, J., Dong, W., Socher, R., Li, L.-J., Li, K., & Fei-Fei, L. (2009). ImageNet: A Large-Scale Hierarchical Image Database. Proceedings of the IEEE/CVF Conference on Computer Vision and Pattern Recognition (CVPR).

Croce, F., Andriushchenko, M., Sehwag, V., et al. (2021). RobustBench: A Standardized Adversarial Robustness Benchmark. Proceedings of the Neural Information Processing Systems Track on Datasets and Benchmarks (NeurIPS).

Secure Multi-Party Computation

Yao, A. C. (1982). Protocols for Secure Computations. Proceedings of the Annual Symposium on Foundations of Computer Science (FOCS).

Goldreich, O. (2004). Foundations of Cryptography: Volume 2, Basic Applications. Cambridge University Press.

www.ingramcontent.com/pod-product-compliance
Lightning Source LLC
LaVergne TN
LVHW102226300926
849160LV00005B/39